A Contractor's Guide to the FIDIC Conditions of Contract

Michael D. Robinson

Independent Consulting Engineer

Companion website is at **www.wiley.com/go/robinsonfidic** and offers invaluable resources for the site-based contractor to freely download and adapt: model form for submissions to the engineer for approval and/or consent; model form of daywork/daily record sheets; and sample model letters for use by the contractor.

WILEY-BLACKWELL

A John Wiley & Sons, Ltd., Publication

This edition first published 2011
© 2011 by John Wiley & Sons, Ltd

Wiley-Blackwell is an imprint of John Wiley & Sons, formed by the merger of Wiley's global Scientific, Technical and Medical business with Blackwell Publishing.

Registered office: John Wiley & Sons, Ltd, The Atrium, Southern Gate, Chichester, West Sussex, PO19 8SQ, UK

Editorial offices: 9600 Garsington Road, Oxford, OX4 2DQ, UK
The Atrium, Southern Gate, Chichester, West Sussex, PO19 8SQ, UK
2121 State Avenue, Ames, Iowa 50014-8300, USA

For details of our global editorial offices, for customer services and for information about how to apply for permission to reuse the copyright material in this book please see our website at www.wiley.com/wiley-blackwell.

The right of the author to be identified as the author of this work has been asserted in accordance with the UK Copyright, Designs and Patents Act 1988.

Library of Congress Cataloging-in-Publication Data

Robinson, Michael D., consulting engineer.
  A contractor's guide to the FIDIC conditions of contract / Michael D. Robinson.
       p. cm.
  Includes bibliographical references and index.
  ISBN 978-0-4706-5764-5 (hardcover : alk. paper)
  1. Construction contracts. 2. Engineering contracts. 3. Architectural contracts. 4. Standardized terms of contract. I. Title.
  K891.B8R6135 2011
  343′.07869–dc22

                                                                    2010042183

A catalogue record for this book is available from the British Library.

This book is published in the following electronic formats: ePDF 9781119993391; Wiley Online Library 9781119993414; ePub 9781119993407

Set in 10/12 pt Sabon by Toppan Best-set Premedia Limited
Printed and bound in Malaysia by Vivar Printing Sdn Bhd

1 2011

Contents

343.
078
69
ROB

Preface

The Conditions of Contract prepared by FIDIC have for many years had no rival as the standard form of choice for use in the international construction industry.

Traditionally in the standard FIDIC forms the Engineer was given an authoritative role, enabling him to make informed judgements concerning the conduct and execution of projects with a large measure of independence from the Employer. From time to time FIDIC updated these standard forms, continuing to maintain the traditional role of the Engineer, culminating in the 4th Edition 1987 (reprinted 1992).

However, throughout the 1980s and 1990s discernible changes developed in the international construction industry. Employers increasingly became involved in day-by-day administration of projects, thereby restricting the powers of the Engineer to act independently of the parties. The diminution of the power and authority of the Engineer had the effect of disturbing the allocation of risk between the parties and as many contractors perceived, to their disadvantage.

The same period saw a marked increase in the availability of international funding, particularly for infrastructure projects. As a consequence more and more companies, both engineers and contractors, undertook contracts outside their national borders. The international construction industry came of age.

Disputes have long been endemic to the construction industry. The increased participation of more companies of differing nationalities in projects outside their own borders inevitably increased the number of disputes arising for a number of reasons. Contractors were not always familiar with the operation of a FIDIC-based contract. Equally, Employers, well used to their own national systems of contracting practices and law, were faced with having to deal with contracts based on unfamiliar FIDIC forms. As a consequence the number of disputes increased markedly.

A key feature of the dispute-resolution procedure contained in the FIDIC 4th Edition 1987, Sub-Clause 67.1 – 'Engineer's Decision' was the power and authority of the Engineer to make independent judgements. As the independence of the Engineer diminished as a result of the increasing direct involvement of the Employer, the value of the Engineer's decision was increasingly challenged by contractors, with the result that more and more disputes were referred to arbitration.

Few in the construction industry regard arbitration as a satisfactory means of resolving disputes. Arbitration is a lengthy and expensive process which may lead to awards that with a more flexible, realistic approach could have been negotiated without arbitration. A contractor also suffers because he is unable to foresee the outcome of the arbitration and his cash flow is uncertain and damaged as a consequence of lengthy arbitration. Regrettably there are instances of employers preferring to refer some disputes to arbitration to avoid having to make decisions which for political or economic reasons they are unwilling to make themselves.

Against this background FIDIC undertook a major review of their standard forms. Following extensive consultations, a new suite of contract forms was issued in 1999:

CONS   Conditions of Contract for Construction ('The Red Book'), which FIDIC recommends for use on building or engineering works designed by the Employer or by his representative, the Engineer.
P & DB   Conditions of Contract for Plant and Design-Build ('The Yellow Book'), which FIDIC recommends for the provision of electrical and/or mechanical plant and for the design and execution of building or engineering works to be designed by the Contractor in accordance with the Employer's requirements.
EPCT   Conditions of Contract for EPC/Turnkey Projects ('The Silver Book'), which FIDIC recommends for the provision of a process or power plant on a turnkey project.

A fourth contract entitled 'Short Form of Contract' ('The Green Book'), intended for use on contracts involving simple or repetitive work, was also issued by FIDIC. This is not considered further in this book.

In the preparation of the new suite of contracts, FIDIC continued with the use of the English language as the language of interpretation. In retaining the use of the English language, FIDIC took the opportunity to ensure that all of the forms in the new suite were written in modern English and not the 'legalese' English of previous editions. Opening an introductory FIDIC seminar in London in early 2000, the chairman, Christopher Wade, remarked that the new suite of contracts 'had been written by engineers for engineers!' Nonetheless, engineers with a lesser command of the English language have tended to find it more difficult to assimilate the requirements, obligations and duties contained in the FIDIC forms.

The FIDIC forms are arranged in twenty primary clauses, each covering a major topic. For inexperienced personnel (particularly those whose mother-tongue is not the English language) it is often difficult to draw together all the sub-clauses relating to a particular issue. For example, the presentation of an individual claim may require reference not only to the sub-clause that permits the contractor to claim, but potentially also to Sub-Clauses 3.5, 8.4 and 20.1 which are widely separated in the FIDIC forms. In the text of this book cross-references to other relevant clauses or sub-clauses are provided. Nonetheless, it is appropriate that professional users of the FIDIC forms should familiarise themselves with the general philosophy adopted by the FIDIC committee in preparation of the forms.

This book has the aim of assisting the contractor's staff to overcome some of the difficulties encountered on a typical international contract using

FIDIC forms. Since the majority of FIDIC-based contracts use 'The Red Book' (CONS), this book concentrates on the use of those particular forms. Supplementary comments are included in Appendix C in respect of 'The Yellow Book' (P & DB), recommended for use where the contractor has a design responsibility. For reasons expressed elsewhere, the third set of forms for turnkey projects, 'The Silver Book' (EPCT), has not found favour. Limited comments are included in Appendix D to this book.

The Contractor is represented on site by the Contractor's Representative who carries the overall responsibility for all the Contractor's on-site activities.

In order to provide guidance to the Contractor's Representative and his staff, this book is divided into sections:

1) A general summarised review of 'The Red Book' from the Contractor's perspective.
2) A review of the activities and duties of the Contractor's Representative in the same clause sequence as they appear in 'The Red Book' with particular reference to submittals to the Employer and the Engineer. Additional notes are included in respect of the activities of the estimating office insofar as they impact on the activities of the Contractor's Representative.
3) A summarised version of the matters referred to in 2), but arranged in order of their likely time sequence on site. This has the added intention of providing the Contractor's Representative with a means of ensuring that documents are not only properly provided to the Employer and Engineer, but most importantly that they are provided within the time limits specified in the Contract.
4) A number of appendices relating to construction topics are provided. These include an appendix containing a selection of model letters on various issues which require the Contractor to make formal submissions to the Employer or Engineer.

This book is intended to provide on-site guidance to the Contractor's Representative and his staff. It is not intended to be a review of the legal aspects of FIDIC-based contracts. Legal advice should be obtained as and when necessary, particularly if the Contractor has little or no knowledge of the local law. It is hoped that this book will assist contractors (and hopefully engineers in supervisory roles) to prevent problems arising rather than spend considerable time and energy resolving those problems once they have arisen. This comment has particular reference to the ever-present issue of resolving claims presented by the Contractor in a timely and professional manner. This book contains only brief quotations from the various FIDIC standard forms. It is recommended that the reader gives consideration to the purchase of a copy of 'The FIDIC Contracts Guide' published by FIDIC in 2000. The publication provides important guidance on the use and interpretation of the referenced FIDIC forms.

Acknowledgements

The author is grateful to the Fédération Internationale des Ingénieurs-Conseils (FIDIC) for permission to quote extracts from the Conditions of Contract for Construction ('The Red Book') and the FIDIC Contracts Guide. All quoted extracts from these publications are given in italics wherever they occur.

In this book, the Employer, the Engineer, the Contractor and Subcontractors are referred to in the masculine gender in conformity with standard FIDIC practice. The author wishes to emphasise that the book is intended to address female readers on an equal basis with their male colleagues and that the use of the masculine gender is for practical reasons only.

Dedication

This book is dedicated to Stewart, Fred, Keith, Fritz and many others who have encouraged me to complete the task of writing this book during its long gestation and to my wife Monika without whose practical help and encouragement nothing would have been achieved.

Review of the FIDIC Conditions of Contract for Construction (CONS) – 'The Red Book'

Clause 1 General Provisions

1.1   Definitions

This sub-clause provides definitions of approximately 65 words and expressions that are used in the Conditions of Contract. With the exception of the words 'day' and 'year', these defined words and expressions are identifiable by the use of capital initial letters.

Consequently, in any submission or correspondence it is important to use the capitalised form of the words and expressions if that is what is precisely intended by the writer.

The FIDIC Contract Guide (p. 339–346) provides a glossary (dictionary) of words and phrases that are in common use in the fields of building consultancy, engineering and associated activities. This glossary is not intended to amplify or replace the definitions given in this Sub-Clause 1.1, but the use of the provided definitions is useful to ensure clarity on a given topic.

Nonetheless, there are a number of words and expressions used in these FIDIC Conditions of Contract that are neither defined in this sub-clause nor yet explained in the glossary. These words and expressions include 'claim', 'event', 'circumstance'. It is logical that these words and expressions have the meanings attached to them from any recognised standard dictionary of the English language (e.g. Oxford, Webster's).

The Parties should take every care to avoid incorporating additional words and expressions of significance into the contract documents without providing a corresponding definition. To illustrate this point, the author has experience of a Red Book contract which required the Contractor to produce 'working drawings'. No definition of 'working drawings' was provided in the contract documents. The Contractor took a broad view that 'working drawings' related to drawings required for his own construction purposes. The Employer sought to extend the responsibility of the Contractor to include correction of elements of a faulty Employer-provided design. A lengthy dispute ensued. The Contractor amended the design under protest. The end result was that the completion was delayed and additional payment eventually became due to the Contractor.

1.2   Interpretation

This sub-clause contains legal statements confirming (except where the context requires otherwise)

(a)   *words indicating one gender – includes all genders*
(b)   *words indicating the singular also include the plural* and vice-versa
(c)   'Agreements' *have to be recorded in writing.* As a consequence the Parties are required to ensure that any verbal agreements are formalised

A Contractor's Guide to the FIDIC Conditions of Contract, First Edition. Michael D. Robinson.
© 2011 John Wiley & Sons, Ltd. Published 2011 by John Wiley & Sons, Ltd.

in writing. Too often important instructions and decisions are not formally recorded by the Parties.

(d)   where something is stated to be '*written*' or '*in writing*' this shall result in a permanent record. This requirement may have consequences in respect of the authorised means of communication identified in Sub-Clause 1.3.

1.3   Communications

This sub-clause identifies the authorised methods of communications between the Parties. Importantly Sub-Clause 1.3(a) provides for the '*use of any agreed systems of electronic transmission between the Parties as stated in the Appendix to Tender*'. If this is not so stated in the Appendix to Tender and the Parties are agreeable to the use of e-mails, then a supplementary agreement between the Employer and Contractor will be required. The difficulty with the use of e-mails is that the sender may not be able to evidence directly if the required recipient did in fact receive the e-mail – this in contrast to telefax messages wherein the recipient's telefax machine does respond. Many e-mail operating systems do provide for electronic receipt of incoming e-mails but this relies on the cooperation of the recipient. In all cases where electronic transmissions are acceptable, it is advisable for confirmatory hard copies of all e-mails to be sent to the recipient at prescribed intervals. In all cases the use of a formal mail transmission book is highly recommended.

Both Parties should ensure that only authorised staff members formally communicate, particularly by e-mail, and that the other Party is informed in writing of the limitations of any delegated authority.

1.4   Law and Language

Both the applicable law and the language of communication are to be defined in the contract documents.

Invariably the applicable law is that of the country where the contract is to be executed. This more so, if the Employer is also resident in that country. Even if the applicable law is not that of the country of execution, it may happen that the local courts will claim jurisdiction regardless of the wording of the contract. Legal advice should be sought should such a situation arise.

Frequently the Employer may require that correspondence addressed to him be written in his own language. Given the vagaries of site translations, it is recommended that correspondence to the Employer and other public bodies be provided simultaneously in both the language of the contract and the local language.

1.5   Priority of Documents

The basic priority listing of the documents forming the contract is given in this sub-clause. Frequently additional documents will be added to the given listing by the Employer prior to tender date.

Preferred tenderers are often invited by the Employer to a post-tender meeting to finalise outstanding issues arising from the Contractor's tender. As a consequence a document entitled 'Minutes of Post-Tender Meeting(s)' or similar is drawn up and is usually accorded highest priority, even above the Conditions of Contract. Both Parties should ensure that the quality of such minute-keeping is of the highest order and that the contents are formally agreed before inclusion in the final Contract Document. Occasionally the Employer may wish to include the Contractor's tender offer in the final Contract Document. Care should be taken to ensure that the Contractor's tender offer, if included, is given the appropriate priority and does not inappropriately contradict the intended priorities of other documents that also form part of the Contract. Sub-Clause 1.1.19 defines 'Appendix to Tender'. There are more than thirty references contained in the Conditions of Contract to the Appendix to Tender. The Appendix to Tender contains specific data qualifying the general data that is provided in the Conditions of Contract. The Appendix to Tender is not shown in the documents listed in this sub-clause. However, most Employers do include the Appendix to Tender as a separate document that is stated to be of higher priority than the Particular Conditions of Contract. It is important that the Contractor carefully checks the data given in the Appendix to Tender to ensure that any impact on his Tender is correctly evaluated. If in the Contractor's opinion the data is incorrect or otherwise not conforming to the General Conditions, then clarification should be sought from the Engineer in the pre-tender period.

The author has experience of a contract where the Percentage for Adjustment of Provisional Sums, (refer to Sub-Clause 13.5 (b)), was left blank by the Employer. Despite the protestations of the Contractor it was later judged that he had accepted a nil percentage and that he was not entitled to any payment under this heading.

1.6   Contract Agreement

The FIDIC 1999 Conditions of Contract envisage that the Employer will provide the Contractor with a Letter of Acceptance as described in Sub-Clause 1.1.1.3, which the Contractor should acknowledge with the date of receipt noted. From the date of receipt of the Letter of Acceptance a binding contractual relationship exists between the Parties. Within 28 days from the date of receipt of the Letter of Acceptance by the Contractor, the Parties are required to enter into a Contract Agreement based on a standard form annexed to the Particular Conditions of Contract. Should there be no Letter of Acceptance, then a Contract Agreement is necessary.

In many jurisdictions it is required that the full Contract documentation, including the Contract Agreement and those documents described in Sub-Clause 1.5, are all brought together in one comprehensive document and signed by the Parties. Only then does the Contract come into force.

To summarise, three possibilities exist for the establishment of a formal contractual relationship:

- the issue of a Letter of Acceptance **or**
- the signing of a Contract Agreement with or without a Letter of Acceptance **or**
- the signing of a formal comprehensive 'Contract' document which would include the Contract Agreement.

The precise method of formalising the Contract is important because it affects other matters under the Contract. For example, the Performance Security, Sub-Clause 4.2, shall be provided by the Contractor within 28 days after receipt of the Letter of Acceptance.

1.7   Assignment

'*Neither Party is permitted to assign or transfer the whole or any part of the Contract or any benefit or interest in or under the Contract without the agreement of the other Party.*' Exceptionally either Party may, as security, assign its right to any money due under the Contract to a bank or financial institution. Not infrequently a government may transfer responsibility for the Contract from one government department to another. Provided the Contract is between the government and the Contractor, this would not be regarded as an assignment. More and more responsibilities are being transferred by governments to government-owned parastatal companies as a prelude to denationalisation. Should this situation arise in mid-contract, then the Contractor should review the risk case by case and obtain legal advice where appropriate.

1.8   Care and Supply of Documents

The Employer is required to provide to the Contractor two copies of the Contract and subsequent drawings. The Contractor has to supply six copies of the Contractor's Documents to the Engineer. The Contractor's Documents would importantly include submittals requiring the Engineer's Consent. The Contractor should seek clarification from the Engineer if a full submittal of all six copies is required at the submittal-for-approval stage. It may be that only a full submittal is required once the documents are approved. It may be mutually convenient if documentation, particularly drawings, can be passed electronically between the Parties. This should be discussed between the Parties at the earliest opportunity as this, for example, would facilitate the production of 'as built' drawings.

1.9   Delayed Drawings and Instructions

The Contractor is required to give notice to the Engineer whenever '*the Works are likely to be delayed or disrupted*' by a delay in the issue of drawings or other instructions by the Employer and/or Engineer as the case may be. The Contractor is further required to provide details of 'who, when and why' the drawings or other instructions are needed. This has a direct relationship to the preparation of programmes (Sub-Clause 8.3 refers). This appears to be an unnecessarily complex procedure, since if the supply of the drawings or instructions is not the Contractor's responsibility, then the responsibility for delay automatically belongs to the Employer. The date by which a drawing or instruction is required can be identified from the contract programme. Particularly on projects where, for example, materials are to be obtained by the Contractor from outside the country of execution, it is not unreasonable to advise the Engineer that all necessary drawings and instructions are required two months or more before the programmed date of execution. Such an agreement also helps the Engineer to plan his own activities, particularly if his own design office is to provide the drawings and instructions. Should the Contractor experience a delay or incur additional costs, he is entitled by reference to this clause and to Sub-Clause 20.1 to give notice of claim to the Engineer.

1.10   Employer's Use of the Contractor's Documents

Although the Contractor retains the copyright and other intellectual property rights in the Contractor's Documents, the Employer has a free licence to use this information for the operation and maintenance of the relevant portion of the Works. It is of interest to note that such free licence does not specifically entitle the Employer to use the Contractor's Documents for publicity or advertising purposes.

The same requirements will apply to the Contractor's Subcontractors and appropriate provisions will have to be included in any Subcontractor's Documents.

1.11   Contractor's Use of Employer's Documents

The Contractor is entitled to use the Employer's Documents solely for the purpose of executing the Contract and for no other purpose without the written permission of the Employer.

1.12   Confidential Details

The Contractor is entitled to keep confidential anything considered a trade secret, but is required to provide sufficient information to verify compliance with the Contract and to comply with the laws of the country of execution.

1.13   Compliance with Statutes, Regulations and Laws

The Employer is required to obtain planning permissions for the Permanent Works and any other permissions where so stated in the Contract. If in doubt, clarification should be requested by the Contractor during the tender phase.

The Contractor is required to give notices, obtain all permits (assumed to include building permits) and licences as required by Contract or Law.

Again, these requirements should be clarified during the tender stage, not least because the Contractor is liable for all costs incurred.

1.14   Joint and Several Liability

The issue of joint and several liability is normally addressed in the Tender Documents. Appropriate documentation is provided with the Tender Documents for completion by tenderers.

Many projects are undertaken by Joint Ventures comprising two or more companies. In the event that one or more of the joint ventures is declared insolvent or is otherwise unable to contribute to the performance of the Contract, then a greater responsibility falls on the surviving partners, who are obliged to continue with the Contract. Self-evidently, the selection of competent, financially stable partners is a crucial aspect of the pre-tender period.

Clause 2 The Employer

2.1   Right of Access to Site

This sub-clause refers not only to the Contractor's Right of Access to the Site, but also to his right to take possession of the Site.

It is intended that the relevant dates for taking possession are to be given in the Appendix to the Tender. If no date(s) is given in the Appendix to the Tender, then the Employer shall provide access to and possession of the Site in accordance with the requirements of the programme that the Contractor is required to submit in accordance with the provisions of Sub-Clause 8.3. In such case the prudent Contractor should show the required handover date or dates in his programme. In any event the handover or part handover cannot be delayed by more than 42 days after the issue of the Letter of Acceptance (refer to Sub-Clause 8.1), otherwise the Commencement Date will be correspondingly delayed. Should a delay occur, the Contractor is entitled to claim both time and costs by reference to this clause and to Clause 20.1.

Importantly, the Employer may delay the handover until the Contractor provides the Performance Security required by Sub-Clause 4.2. Additionally, the Employer understandably may be reluctant to allow the Contractor to commence work without appropriate insurances in place.

The handover of the Site is a significant event and should be properly managed. It is the Employer's duty to hand over the Site, not the Engineer's. The Contractor should inspect the site carefully and investigate any potential obstructions including those that may not be his contractual responsibility. Typically, an empty, unsecured site is a magnet for third parties, who illegally dump waste after the tender site inspection and before commencement. Equally, delays may occur because requisitioned properties have not been vacated due to a lack of compensation payments.

A formal protocol should be drawn up, identifying not only the date/timing of the handover, but also the result of the site inspection. This protocol is to be signed by authorised representatives of both the Employer and Contractor.

For partial handovers a protocol is required for each handover.

Frequently the Contractor may agree to accept the site even though there exist obstructions that are the responsibility of the Employer. A most common cause of obstruction arises from the lack of, or incomplete, land requisition. If these are restricted to small areas, the protocol should indicate the dates by which the handover will be finally achieved.

Although it is laudable to commence physical work as soon as possible, it is frequently not in the Contractor's interest to commence work in a fragmented, inefficient manner. It may be appropriate for the Contractor to decline an incomplete handover and make claim as permitted under this sub-clause of the Contract.

In addition to handing over the Site, the Employer is also required to grant the Contractor the right of access to the Site. It is assumed that there already exists a suitable route or one that can be constructed by the Contractor. Under Sub-Clause 4.15 the Contractor is deemed to have satisfied himself in this matter. Having been granted a right of access, the Contractor assumes the risk for all practical difficulties (and costs) in providing the access. This is clearly an issue that the Contractor is required to have carefully reviewed during the pre-tender site inspection.

Exceptionally, the Site may be surrounded by land owned by third parties. The Employer remains responsible to ensure that a viable access is possible. In such instances the issue of access to the Site should be clarified in the pre-tender period.

It should not be assumed that because the site is owned by the Employer – possibly a government department – and the surrounding land by another government department, this will necessarily ensure unrestricted access to the site. For example, there may be security restrictions, particularly in the vicinity of airports and military installations.

2.2   Permits, Licences or Approvals

Frequently the assistance of the Employer is required to enable the Contractor to obtain the various permits, licences and approvals necessary for the performance of the Contract.

The nature of the required permits, licences and approvals will vary from country to country and from project to project and could include building permits, trade licences, licences for quarry operations, approvals from utility companies. These requirements should be researched using local knowledge and their potential value and impact on the timely performance of the Works evaluated in the preparation of the tender.

It may be appropriate to raise any concerns during pre-tender meetings, so that the commitment of the Employer to assist in resolving problems is well established. Typical problems that frequently occur include:

- In many countries with a policy of centralised planning the supply of basic materials (cement, bitumen, fuels etc.) may be strictly controlled and bulk supplies only available with the support of the Employer. Even then the authorities are often unwilling to pre-advise of any supply bottlenecks, which can be extremely frustrating.
- Many projects are stated to be free of local taxes. Of particular interest are customs duties and value added tax (VAT). Often these arrangements cause problems between one state ministry (e.g. the Treasury ministry controlling the collection of taxes and revenues) and the Employer. Important supplies and equipment can be held up in part because the Treasury Department has failed to issue internal authorisation for duty-free imports. The Contractor (unless required by law) should not pay temporary deposits unless the Employer acknowledges liability to arrange for a refund. It is often very difficult to obtain refunds from Treasury Departments. Again, during any pre-tender meeting the Employer could be asked to confirm that the appropriate arrangements are in hand. An unforeseen need to pay customs duties even on a temporary basis can affect the Contractor's cash flow which can be damaging in the early stages of a contract.

- In many countries utility companies are tardy in dealing with requests for relocation of services, frequently because of a lack of material or skilled workers and occasionally because of a reluctance to deal expediently with requests from a contractor without local connections.

2.3 Employer's Personnel

The Employer is responsible to ensure that his personnel support the Contractor's efforts in respect of general cooperation and specifically Safety Procedures and Protection of Environment.

2.4 Employer's Financial Arrangement

'*The Employer shall submit, within 28 days after receiving any request from the Contractor, reasonable evidence that financial arrangements have been made and are being maintained which will enable the Employer to pay the Contract Price …*'.

Should the Employer finance the Works from his own sources, it may be difficult to produce the 'reasonable evidence' required by this sub-clause. However, if the Employer is an agency of a stable government, concerns will be minimised. A considerable number of contracts are financed by external financing of known provenance and the risk of non-payment can be assessed. Other financing is provided by international aid and finance organisations to Governments for specific projects with a fixed budget. The Contractor should be continuously aware of the financial status of his contract in order to be assured that sufficient funds are available to pay for all work instructed. Such calculations should take into account the likely value of outstanding claims and the financial implications of other unresolved items. If the Employer is unable or unwilling to provide the required evidence when requested by the Contractor, the Contractor would be entitled to take action as described in Clause 16 'Suspension and Termination by the Contractor'. Should doubts remain that the existing funding is likely to be inadequate, it would be politic for the Contractor to discuss his concerns with the Employer ahead of any formal correspondence.

2.5 Employer's Claims

This sub-clause entitles the Employer to make formal claims against the Contractor. The Employer has broadly to follow the same procedure adopted for claims by the Contractor against the Employer. The Employer has to give notice of claim '*as soon as practical after which (he) became aware of the event or circumstances giving rise to claim*'. This contrasts with the 28-day time limit imposed by Sub-Clause 20.1 in respect of Contractor's claims against the Employer. There is no precise definition of the time span intended by the wording '*as soon as practical …*'.

The Employer is to provide detailed particulars and substantiation of the amount to which he considers himself entitled.

Chapter 1

The Engineer has the duty to agree or determine the claim in accordance with the provision of Sub-Clause 3.5. A full listing of clauses giving rise to the right for the Employer to make claims against the Contractor is given in Appendix B. Possibly the most significant of these potential claim headings are those given in Sub-Clause 8.7 'Delay Damages'.

Clause 3 The Engineer

3.1   Engineer's Duties and Authority

This sub-clause confirms the fundamental obligation of the Employer to appoint the Engineer to carry out the duties assigned to him in the Contract. The Engineer may be a named person or may be a company. Should a company be named as Engineer, then the company has to advise the name of the person who will specifically be allocated the duties of the Engineer.

The Engineer is frequently named in the Tender Documents, which allows the Contractor to assess the potential risk involved in this appointment. Less satisfactory is the appointment of the Engineer in the post-tender period prior to the Commencement Date. For the Contract to properly function, the Engineer needs to be available by the Commencement Date. Usually if no Engineer is appointed, the Employer invariably seeks to appoint one of his own staff as Engineer on a temporary basis. Self-evidently, such an appointee cannot be considered as an independent Engineer. In such circumstances the Contractor should give careful consideration to the implication of such an interim appointment. The temporary appointment should be accepted only for a very limited period by the Contractor.

The duties and authority allocated to the Engineer are given in the various clauses of the Contract. However, it is now standard practice for these duties and authority to be varied by amended clauses included in the Particular Conditions of Contract. Routinely, the Engineer is not allowed to authorise additional expenditure (except possibly minor amounts), nor to authorise extensions of time, nor to issue Taking Over Certificates or the Performance Certificate without the consent of the Employer. These limitations can be quite frustrating because the direct involvement of the Employer frequently delays the administration process of the Contract to the Contractor's disadvantage.

Sub-Clause 3.1(a) clarifies 'that the Engineer whenever carrying out his duties or exercising authority … the Engineer shall be deemed to act for the Employer'. The time-honoured concept of the Engineer acting according to his own independent experience and skills is no longer valid.

Further, Sub-Clause 3.1(b) confirms 'that the Engineer has no authority to relieve either Party of any duties, obligations or responsibilities under the Contract except as stated in the Contract'. The principal exception is the right of the Engineer to instruct variations because they may include omission of any work (refer to Sub-Clause 13.1(d)), but this may be amended in the Particular Conditions of Contract.

For illustrative purposes, it may happen that some constructed part of the Work does not conform to the technical requirements of the Contract. The Engineer has no authority to vary the technical requirements to accommodate the nonconformity. Acceptance of the nonconformance even with price adjustment would require the concurrence of the Employer.

Finally, Sub-Clause 3.1(c) confirms that 'any approval or similar (including absence of disapproval) by the Engineer does not relieve the Contractor from any responsibility he may have under the Contract'. Thus, if a part of the Works previously approved or accepted by the Engineer is later found to be defective or nonconforming, the Contractor is still obligated to make good the defect or nonconformance at his own expense.

Importantly, it is to be noted that when the Contractor receives an Engineer's communication for which the Employer's prior approval was required, the Contractor is not entitled to query whether it was approved. The Employer is deemed to have given approval. Notwithstanding, a prudent contractor should find an informal route to ensure that the Employer has indeed given his consent, particularly in respect of important issues. Any subsequent disputes consequent upon such communication are to be dealt with between the Employer and the Engineer.

3.2   Delegation by the Engineer

The Engineer is authorised to delegate authority to assistants such as Resident Engineers, inspectors, laboratory engineers and similar. However, the Engineer is not permitted *'to delegate the authority to determine any matter in accordance with Sub-Clause 3.5 (Determinations)'*. Engineers, experienced with FIDIC-based contracts, routinely provide the Contractor with the names and positions of his appointed assistants and the authority delegated to them. It is important that the Contractor's key staff are familiar with this information.

Sub-Clause 3.2(b) permits the Contractor to refer the determination or instruction of an assistant of the Engineer to the Engineer for confirmation or reversal.

One important consequence of this process of delegation is that some communications will need to be sent to the Engineer in respect of non-delegated matters, and other communications sent to the Engineer's assistant(s) where authority is delegated. Claim notifications under Clause 20.1 will invariably have to be sent to the Engineer, whereas applications for Interim Payment Certificates will most likely be sent to the Engineer's principal site assistant (e.g. the Resident Engineer) for further action. Should there be any doubt whether a communication should be sent to the Engineer or to one of his assistants, then – as a protective measure – the communication could be sent to both parties simultaneously.

3.3   Instructions of the Engineer

'The Contractor shall only take instructions from the Engineer or his delegated assistant.' This sub-clause further states that *'if an instruction constitutes a Variation, Clause 13 (Variations and Adjustments) shall apply.'* However, if the Particular Conditions of Contract, Clause 3.1, are amended to prevent the Engineer issuing additional or varied work involving additional cost without the agreement of the Employer, there arises a conflict.

Consequently, if the Engineer or a delegated assistant issues an instruction representing a variation with additional costs, the Contractor is advised to immediately draw the attention of the Engineer to the problem, so that a resolution is speedily found. This hypothetical situation is contradictory, because the Contractor has a general duty to conform to the legal instructions of the Engineer.

Should it not be possible to resolve the matter in a short time, the Contractor should consider giving notice of claim under Clause 20.1 to prevent any possibility of a potential claim being time barred.

The Engineer or his delegated assistants may give instructions orally or in writing.

In the event of oral instructions, the Contractor should consider the necessity of confirming in writing the Engineer's instruction within a 2-day time limit. The Engineer then has a further 2 days to confirm or reject the instruction, otherwise the instruction is automatically confirmed.

The Contractor should consider which members of his workforce (other than the Contractor's Representative) shall be authorised to receive instructions from the Engineer or his delegated assistant(s). This is a fine judgement, since direct discussions (even if interpreted as instructions) between the Engineer's field inspectors and the Contractor's foremen are an essential feature of any construction site.

As a guide it is recommended that the Contractor's Representative informs the Engineer that whilst routine instructions may be given to his senior staff members, any instructions involving additional cost or time have to be first referred to the Contractor's Representative (or named assistants) before implementation.

In this respect subcontractors are frequently the source of major communication problems, particularly if the work allocated to subcontractors is a substantial portion of the Works. Subcontractors should not be authorised to receive major instructions directly from the Engineer or his delegated assistant(s) and for most purposes subcontractors should be given only the same level of independence as the equivalent Contractor's staff. Should the Engineer issue formal instructions pertaining to the subcontractors, these should be distributed through the Contractor's office and not directly to the subcontractor.

FIDIC is not concerned with the Contractor's administration of his subcontractors, except in a generalised manner described in Section 4 of the Conditions of Contract, but clearly the Contractor must have adequate controls to manage and discipline subcontractors and ensure correct payment under the terms of the subcontracts.

3.4   Replacement of the Engineer

The Employer is required to give the Contractor not less than 42 days before the intended replacement of the Engineer. The Contractor is entitled to object to the replacement of the Engineer. The objection has to be 'reasonable' and supporting particulars have to be provided.

It is difficult to envisage the circumstance that might give rise to objection by the Contractor. Possibly if the replacement Engineer and the Contractor have had a bad relationship on a previous project, it might be unwise of the Employer to risk extending adverse relationships into another project.

However, it is a fact that many Employers, because of their own procurement rules, have effectively engaged the replacement Engineer before advising the Contractor. It is submitted that this sub-clause does not suit the purpose for which it was intended.

3.5   Determinations

Clauses permitting the Contractor to claim additional payment or extended time for completion are distributed throughout the Conditions of Contract. The various clauses that entitle the Contractor to claim are listed in Appendix A.

Sub-Clause 20.1 describes in detail the procedure to be followed by the Contractor, should he consider himself entitled to additional payment, an extension of time, or both. It is crucial that the Contractor adheres to the time limitations given in that sub-clause.

Provided that the Contractor has correctly followed the procedural requirements of Sub-Clause 20.1, the Engineer is required to respond within the fixed time limits (also stated in Sub-Clause 20.1) with approval or disapproval and detailed comments.

Sub-Clause 3.5 requires the Engineer to agree or determine any matter under the Contract and is the formal response to any claim raised by the Contractor.

It shall be noted that Sub-Clause 3.2 prohibits the Engineer from delegating his obligations under this sub-clause.

In respect of Sub-Clause 3.1 'Engineer's Duties and Authority', it was noted that the authority of the Engineer is frequently amended in the Particular Conditions of Contract. Specifically, the Engineer is not permitted to authorise additional payment without the prior agreement of the Employer. Consequently, there is potential conflict between the Engineer's obligations contained in Sub-Clauses 3.5 and 20.1 and the Particular Conditions of Contract. It may be assumed that the Engineer will not make a determination awarding additional payment or an extension of time to the Contractor without having obtained the prior agreement of the Employer.

The FIDIC guide recommends that if the Engineer is an independent consulting engineer who is to act impartially, the following should be added at the end of the first paragraph of Sub-Clause 3.5: '... *The Engineer shall act impartially when making these determinations*'. Such wording will negate any restrictions placed on the Engineer in authorising additional payments to the Contractor.It is most unusual for the Engineer to be granted such independence. The FIDIC Guide summarises the procedures to be followed by the Engineer in preparing his determination. The Engineer is firstly required to consult with both Parties, separately or jointly, and make every effort to achieve the agreement of both Parties and not with one Party only. If the agreement of both Parties cannot be achieved within a reasonable period of time, the Engineer is then required to make a '*fair determination in accordance with the Contract*' which he has then to notify to the Parties. This determination is binding upon both Parties unless revised under the DAB procedure (refer to Clause 20). It is quite possible that the Engineer will issue an interim determination with the intention to finalise the matter if and when more detailed particulars become available.

Clause 4 The Contractor

4.1   Contractor's General Obligations

This sub-clause describes in broad detail the general obligations of the Contractor.

The Contractor is required to:

- '*design (to the extent specified in the Contract), execute and complete the Works.*' The extent of the Contractor's involvement in design should be clearly expressed in the Contract Documents. Any lack of clarity should be queried in the Tender period. The Engineer is responsible for the coordination of designs.
- provide all manpower, plant and materials, whether of permanent or temporary nature, required for the design, execution and completion of the Works including remedying the defects.
- take responsibility for adequacy, stability and safety of all Site operations. The Contractor will submit details of all arrangements (e.g. plant and office layouts) and methods of execution ('Method Statements').
- follow specified procedures for the submittal of Contractor's Documents for any part of the Permanent Works designed by the Contractor. Further, the Contractor is requested to submit 'as built' documents together with operation and maintenance manuals.

The Contractor has no responsibility for the Engineer's design and specifications, including subsequent changes introduced by the Engineer during the construction stage.

Frequently the Contractor has to provide the name and particulars of the Contractor's Representative with his tender. Difficulties can arise because the proposed person may subsequently leave the employment of the Contractor or, as not infrequently is the case, is no longer available because the award and subsequent commencement of the Works are significantly delayed. In such event the Contractor is required to submit the '*name and particulars of another suitable person ...*' for the position.

The appointment of the Contractor's Representative is an important event of contractual significance. The Contractor should ensure that in addition to his formal appointment he is correctly introduced to both the Employer and the Engineer. Similarly, if the Contractor's Representative is to be replaced or withdraws, the Employer and the Engineer should be informed in order that the appointment of the replacement can follow smoothly without disappointment to either Party.

It has to be recognised that regardless of the definitive statements contained in the Contract, neither the Employer nor the Engineer nor the Contractor will allow delegation of powers to their representatives that will endanger or destabilise their commercial or legal interests.

The Contractor's Representative can delegate any powers or authority to any 'competent person'. This has parallels to delegation of powers or authority by the Engineer to a delegated assistant (cross-refer to Sub-Clause 3.2).

Chapter 1

The Contractor's Representative should approach this subject most carefully with particular reference to Sub-Clause 1.3 'Communications'.

4.2 Performance Security

The Contractor is required to provide to the Employer (not the Engineer) at his own cost a Performance Security within 28 days after receiving the Letter of Acceptance. The Employer (not the Engineer) is required to give written approval which shall be not unreasonably withheld (cross-refer to Clause 1.3).

The amount and currency of the Performance Security shall be stated in the Appendix to Tender. '*If an amount is not stated in the Appendix to the Tender, then no performance security is required.*'

The Performance Security has to be provided '*by an entity approved by the Employer and shall be in accordance with a standard form annexed to the Particular Conditions*'. There are two types of Performance Security – an unconditional security that may be called on demand without pre-conditions and which is favoured by employers; and a conditional security that requires certain conditions to be satisfied before it may be called. This latter type provides less scope for unfair calls. In some jurisdictions the unconditional type is no longer permitted by law.

The Performance Security is to remain valid until the Contractor has executed and completed the Works which would give an expiry date corresponding to the anticipated Completion Date (and not the date of Taking Over described in Sub-Clauses 10.1 and 10.2).

4.3 Contractor's Representative

The Contractor shall appoint the Contractor's Representative (frequently referred to as the Site Manager, Site Agent or similar) and shall give him all authority to act on the Contractor's behalf for the performance of the Contract. The Contractor's Representative and his key staff shall be fluent in the language for communications defined in Sub-Clause 1.4. The provision of interpreters by the Contractor may be obligatory.

4.4 Subcontractors

The Contractor is not entitled to subcontract the whole of the Works. A limit to the amount that can be delegated may be given in the Contract Documents. It is possible that the Employer or Engineer may from time to time require evidence of compliance.

'*The Contractor is responsible for the acts and defaults of the Subcontractors (including his agents and employees) as if they were acts and defaults of the Contractor.*'

The Contractor is required to obtain prior consent of the Engineer to subcontract parts of the Works with the proviso that no approval is required in respect of suppliers of materials or subcontractors who are named in the Contract.

There are administrative advantages to be gained by the Contractor if he can identify at least key subcontractors and suppliers in his tender offer. However, these advantages have to be balanced against the reliability of the subcontractor and his willingness to give financial commitments far in advance of the actual performance of the subcontract works.

A tender requirement for Contractors to specify their subcontractors can give rise to difficulties in some Middle-Eastern countries, where the business culture is different from that in the West. Having been awarded a contract for which it was obligatory to name his subcontractors, the Contractor is placed in considerable difficulty if those subcontractors decline to enter into a formal subcontract or take advantage of the situation by significantly increasing their tender offers. The Contractor often will find it difficult and time-consuming to obtain the agreement of the Employer to change the subcontractor, since this most likely will lead to technical changes. The natural suspicion is that the Contractor wishes to change subcontractors for his own financial benefit. A considerable effort may be required to allay the concerns of the Employer. This can be complex since the Contractor may be required to provide a technical comparison between subcontractors' products. Should the two subcontractors' suppliers use different national technical standards, then the comparison is made even more onerous.

Clearly, if the Contractor is obliged or wishes to identify his proposed subcontractors in his tender offer, he should make every effort to deal with reputable subcontractors, especially those with whom he has dealt with previously. Consideration could be given to the use of the pre-bid agreements, whereby the subcontractor is guaranteed work at a fixed price should the tender of the Contractor be accepted.

Ideally, subcontract documents specifying the agreement between the Contractor and the Subcontractor should be back-to-back with those of the Main Contract. This has the advantage that risk-sharing between Contractor and Subcontractor is proportionate to risk inherent in the performance of the Contract.

However, it is frequently the case that the subcontractor may be unable or unwilling to accept all of the shared risk. Consequently the price of the Subcontractor will need to reflect the actual agreed risk-sharing. Risk items to be considered could include the extent to which the Contractor's insurances will also cover the Subcontractor, what site facilities will be provided by the Contractor for the Subcontractor, varied payment terms etc.

In previous FIDIC forms, notably the FIDIC 4th Edition 1987 forms, FIDIC published a standard form of subcontract which was 'back to back' with the standard Conditions of Contract. To date FIDIC has not published a standard form of subcontract for the 1999 forms now under review. Contractors have therefore to provide their own forms of subcontract. The production of a standard form of subcontract can be problematic as the nature and scope of a subcontract can vary enormously. A small, specialist subcontractor from a small town could not be expected to operate a full

Chapter 1

FIDIC-based subcontract, quite probably written in what is to him a foreign language. Equally, a supplier of electrical or mechanical plant would require a different form of subcontract from that of a civil subcontractor working only on the site.

Contractors therefore need to have available a range of differing subcontract forms suitable for most of their activities which can be intelligently modified as required for specific situations.

In this respect nominated Subcontractors, as defined in Clause 5.1, have essentially to accept risk provisions back-to-back with those of the Contract. Whilst the Contractor may operate with a degree of flexibility, he has no obligation to accept a higher risk in respect of nominated Subcontractors. The nominated Subcontractors should be fully aware of their risk and obligations to be included in their offer. The Employer and/or Engineer may have to intervene if the nominated Subcontractor wishes to pass more risk or obligations to the Contractor, since the Contractor is entitled to seek compensatory payment to cover the risk or obligation prior to formalisation of the subcontract.

4.5   Assignment of Benefit of Subcontract

In some circumstances the obligations of the Subcontractor may extend beyond the expiry date of the relevant Defects Notification Period. For example, elevators, air-conditioning units and similar may have to be maintained for a period well in excess of the Defects Notification Period for which the Contractor is liable under the Contract.

Experienced Employers and Engineers are well aware of the need to retain the services of the Subcontractor after the departure of the Contractor from Site. For the most part, Subcontractors welcome the possibility of extended maintenance contracts (or material supply) and are willing to accept the assignment of the benefit of the subcontract to the Employer.

At the time of preparing his tender the Contractor should check if provisions have been included in the tender documents for the assignment of benefit of the Subcontract to the Employer. If there is no such provision, then the Contractor should ask the Engineer to clarify the requirements of the Employer. In any event the issue of assignment has to be included in the subcontract documents.

4.6   Co-operation

This sub-clause requires the Contractor to allow opportunities for the Employer's personnel, other contractors employed by the Employer, and the personnel of public authorities to carry out work.

In principle these works should be identified in the tender documents and the Contractor should make his prices accordingly. These works may have a programming impact and this should also be recorded so that in the event of individual delays, the delay to the Completion Date can be ascertained and responsibility allocated.

Should the degree of the cooperation be extended or enlarged in excess of that identified in the tender documents, the Engineer is required to issue instructions to the Contractor. '*The Engineer's instruction shall constitute a Variation if and to the extent it causes the Contractor to incur Unforeseeable Cost*'. FIDIC is silent in respect of the possibility that the Engineer's instruction may cause delays that would entitle the Contractor to an extension of time. Nonetheless, the Contractor should give notice of claim if such an event occurs.

It is further stated that the services to be provided by the Contractor under this sub-clause may include '*the use of Contractor's Equipment, Temporary Works or access arrangements, which are the responsibility of the Contractor*'.

The use of the Contractor's Equipment by others would entitle the Contractor to corresponding payment. This provision may also disrupt the Contractor's own activities, entitling the Contractor to an extension of time. The Engineer should be requested to adjudicate if there is a conflict.

'Temporary Works or access arrangements' refers to use of scaffolding, access ladders, walkways, access roads already provided by the Contractor for his own use. The Contractor is not obligated to provide additional temporary works or accesses for others. However, he may agree to do so for additional payment.

4.7   Setting Out

The setting-out data may be provided by the Contractor, but is more commonly provided by the Engineer on behalf of the Employer.

The Contractor is responsible for setting out the Works using the provided data and shall notify the Engineer of any errors observed during the setting-out operation. If the Contractor incurs additional cost or is delayed as a consequence of incorrect data, he is entitled to an extension of time for any delay together with payment of his additional costs plus reasonable profit.

In addition to a timely notification of his claim, the Contractor is strongly advised to maintain accurate records (preferably in cooperation with the Engineer) of the delays and additional costs incurred.

'*Thereafter the Engineer is required to proceed in accordance with Sub-Clause 3.5 and to agree or determine to what extent the error could not reasonably have been discovered*' and to evaluate the Contractor's entitlement to additional payment and/or an extension of time.

4.8   Safety Procedures

The detail and implementation of safety regulations vary markedly from country to country. The more developed the country of execution, the more detailed are the laws relating to safety requirements likely to be. The laws of the country of execution of the Works will prevail over any obligation given in the Contract.

Owing to this diversity in law and application, FIDIC can only address the issue of safety in a generalised manner.

Most major contractors working in the field of international construction have prepared their own in-house safety manual. Therefore a check must be made to make sure that this manual conforms to local legal requirements and fully addresses the requirements of the Contract.

The Employer and the Engineer because of their physical presence on site also have a contribution to make to site safety.

Therefore it is recommended that a further document be prepared to supplement the Contractor's Standard Safety Manual. This would also take into account local language and local customs' requirements.

The two documents taken together can be considered analogous to the FIDIC General Conditions and Particular Conditions of Contract. Although not identified in the FIDIC standard forms, most contracts do require the appointment of a Safety Officer whose duty is to oversee safety issues. The Safety Officer should report directly to the Contractor's Representative.

4.9   Quality Assurance

'*The Contractor is required to institute a quality assurance system to demonstrate compliance with the requirements of the Contract.*' Many contractors working in the field of international construction will have a standard in-house manual conforming to the requirements of the international standard ISO 9001. If the contract documents do not refer to ISO 9001, the Contractor may choose to confirm his intentions to comply with ISO 9001 as part of his tender submittal. Each contract will have its own particular requirements and the Contractor will need to prepare supplementary documents to demonstrate conformity with those particular requirements. These documents have to be submitted to the Engineer for 'information' (not approval) at each stage of the Contract.

The Engineer is authorised to audit any aspect of the quality-assurance system. Before submitting documentation to the Engineer, the Contractor is required to approve the documentation himself.

ISO 9001 is not yet a standard document in use in all countries. However, in such event the Contractor may yet find it convenient to base his proposals on ISO 9001.

4.10   Site Data

This clause requires that the Employer makes available to the Contractor prior to the Base Date '*all relevant information in the Employer's possession of sub-surface and hydrological conditions at the Site including environmental aspects*'. The Employer may choose to supply this information as part of the Tender documentation or, if the data is bulky, he may invite tenderers to inspect the data at a given location.

The Contractor is responsible for the interpretation of such data.

Other key data may be available from other sources, particularly government offices and agencies. This could include statistical data, indices, labour laws including levels of pay, company law and similar. The Contractor is solely responsible for identifying, collecting and analysing this data. It is a truism that a tenderer given unlimited time and unlimited resources could discover everything necessary for a risk-free project. This is clearly not a practical consideration for a tenderer preparing his offer in a limited period of time. FIDIC recognises this reality by stating that '… *to the extent which was practicable (taking into account of cost and time), the Contractor shall be deemed to have obtained all necessary information* …'.

This criterion of practicality has a profound influence on any claim the Contractor may wish to make under the provisions of Sub-Clause 4.12 'Unforeseeable Physical Conditions'. The Contractor's estimating office would be well advised to keep copies or records of the data provided by the Employer together with copies or records of data obtained elsewhere that had an influence on his tender. These may be important in the evaluation of claims.

Under this sub-clause the '*Contractor is deemed to have inspected and examined the site before submitting his Tender offer*'.

It is not an obligatory duty, but the majority of employers organise a formal inspection of the site which the Contractor may be obliged to attend as a precondition of the tendering process. Should the Site be in a restricted area, the formal inspection may be the only opportunity for the Contractor to inspect the site. It is recommended that the Contractor properly prepare himself for any site inspection. Clarifications should be sought where appropriate from the Employer/Engineer. A written record should be prepared complete with a photographic record for future reference.

Should the Employer come into possession of other data after the Base Date, he is obliged to supply the same to the tenderers for evaluation. It may be that the other Data will lead to claims from the Contractor for additional payment. However, if the Employer negligently or intentionally withholds data, he may leave himself exposed to legal actions, especially in the event of death or injury or loss during the execution of the Works.

4.11   Sufficiency of the Accepted Contract Amount

'*The Contractor is deemed to have satisfied himself as to the correctness and sufficiency of the Accepted Contract Amount and have based the Accepted Contract Amount on the matters referred to in Sub-Clause 4.10 "Site Data"* '.

4.12   Unforeseeable Physical Conditions

If the Contractor encounters adverse physical conditions which he considers to have been 'Unforeseeable', he shall give notice to the Engineer, with copy to the Employer, and shall be entitled to an extension of time and payment of any cost arising as a consequence of the unforeseeable physical conditions.

'Unforeseeable' is defined in Sub-Clause 1.1.6.8 as meaning 'not reasonably foreseeable by an experienced contractor by the date for submission of the Tender'. It will be noted that the definition given refers to a hypothetical experienced contractor and not to the Contractor himself. In the presentation of any claim under this heading, the Contractor's logic should be to demonstrate that a typically experienced contractor could not have foreseen the unforeseeable condition and therefore he, the Contractor, also an experienced contractor, would equally not have foreseen the unforeseeable condition. What the Contractor himself may or may not have foreseen is not of immediate concern.

Frequently secondary disputes may arise over the practical application of the word 'reasonably' contained in Sub-Clause 1.1.6.8. In attempting to provide guidance on this point, the FIDIC Guide expresses the opinion that for a contract of three years' duration an experienced contractor might be expected to foresee an event which occurs on average once every six years. An event which occurs once every ten years might be regarded as 'unforeseeable'. Another authority has commented that the reference is to what was reasonably foreseeable by an experienced contractor and not by a research professor at university.

Secondly, the cut-off date for foreseeability is the date of tender and not the Base Date. This criterion appears to be harsh on the Contractor since it implies he has to conduct one last site inspection just before submitting his tender offer, which is clearly impractical.

FIDIC defines physical conditions '*as natural physical conditions and man made or other physical conditions and pollutants which the Contractor encounters at the Site, including sub-surface and hydrological conditions, but excluding climatic conditions*'.

'*Sub-surface conditions*' *are those conditions below the surface, including those with a body of water and those below the river bed or sea bed.*

'*Hydrological conditions*' *means the flows of water, including those which are attributable to off-Site climatic conditions.*

'*Physical conditions*' *excludes climatic conditions at the Site and therefore excludes the hydrological consequences of climatic conditions at Site.*

The foregoing leads to the following basic procedure in dealing with claims under Clause 4.12 Unforeseeable Physical Conditions.

- In the preparation of his claim submittal, the Contractor must first demonstrate unforeseeability (by an experienced contractor), with particular reference to Clause 4.10 'Site Data' and any other data that may be contained elsewhere in the Contract Documents.
- The unforeseeable condition must be encountered at the Site. Unforeseeable conditions off-site do not meet this criterion.
- The unforeseeable condition must be physical and not concerned with administrative events for example.
- Adverse '*climatic conditions on the Site, such as the effect of rainfall*', wind or abnormal temperatures are excluded.
- Adverse hydrological conditions, such as flows of water, are admissible including those attributable to off-site conditions such as flooding from a nearby stream or river.

A significant portion of claims submitted under this sub-clause relate to sub-surface geological conditions, which may require expert opinion in support of the claim. Claims relating to adverse hydrological conditions require an evaluation of the statistical frequency and severity of the unforeseeable event and a demonstration that the frequency and/or severity of the event was not foreseeable by an experienced contractor. This type of unforeseeable event may be covered by some part of the contract insurances, but it should be borne in mind that insurers do not award extensions of time.

Certain extreme categories of natural disasters which could also not been foreseen by an experienced contractor are included in Sub-Clause 19.1 'Definition of Force Majeure'.

Should the Contractor consider that he has encountered an Unforeseen Physical Condition, he is required to give notice to the Engineer in accordance with the 28-day period stated in Sub-Clause 20.1. Except in the most obvious circumstances, it is highly likely that there will be a significant time lapse before the existence of the Unforeseen Physical Condition is recognised by the Engineer (and behind the scenes by the Employer).

The Contractor has a duty to continue with the Works regardless of his claim that he has encountered an Unforeseen Physical Condition.

The FIDIC Guide states that the Contractor '*is expected to use his expertise*' to overcome the adverse conditions. The Engineer should cooperate with the Contractor to identify technical solutions which fulfil the principles of the Engineer's design. This cooperation is important because remedial work or changes to the performance of the Works may in themselves represent Variations and Adjustments as described in Clause 13.

Should the Engineer for whatever reasons decline to participate in the process to find solutions, the Contractor may have to proceed unilaterally. In such case it is vital that he keeps the Engineer informed of the Contractor's proposals which should be supported by adequate technical documentation.

In dealing with the perceived Unforeseen Physical Condition, the Contractor must maintain detailed records of his activities on a day-by-day basis to the Engineer for agreement. The Engineer may decline to agree these records as a basis for payment, but he may be prepared to agree them for 'record purposes only' without any contractual commitment. It would be most unfortunate if there was no response from the Engineer to agree detailed records, as the Contractor would be fully entitled to evaluate any future claim based on those records. DAB and Arbitration boards may take a negative view of non-cooperation.

In the event of a valid claim for Unforeseen Physical Conditions, Sub-Clause 4.12, the Contractor is entitled to payment of (additional) cost incurred as a consequence of overcoming the Unforeseen Physical Condition.

The Contractor is theoretically entitled to payment for the original work at the billed rates (or varied rates) and, in addition, payment of the cost of any additional measures necessary to deal with the Unforeseen Physical Condition. Payments at bill rates include a profit allowance, whereas payment of cost excludes profit.

In practice it may be difficult, if not impractical, for the Contractor to divide the total package of work affected by the Unforeseen Physical Condition into a component of work directly related to the Unforeseen Physical Condition and separately into a component of original work.

Chapter 1

The Contractor may elect to value the total package on the basis of cost, but would then lose the profit element on the original work component. In preparing his records, the Contractor should consider the possibility of separating the two components. Again, this is a topic that could be usefully discussed in advance with the Engineer.

FIDIC has introduced an additional proviso not contained in previous contract forms concerning more favourable conditions. Before any additional cost is finally agreed or determined, the Engineer may (permissively) review whether other physical conditions in similar parts of the Works (if any) were more favourable than could reasonably be foreseen when the Contractor submitted the Tender. It may be presumed that the foreseeability criterion applies to that which could be foreseen by an experienced contractor and does not refer to what the Engineer considers foreseeable.

The above is most likely to apply to projects involving repetitive work – building foundations, machine bases and similar. Should the Engineer determine that the Contractor has received a benefit as a consequence of more favourable conditions, then the cost due elsewhere to the Contractor for proven unforeseeable physical conditions shall be reduced accordingly. This process shall not result in a net reduction in the Contract Price.

Finally, the Engineer in making his determinations may take account of the physical conditions actually foreseen by the Contractor when submitting the Tender. The FIDIC Guide notes that if a dispute arises and is referred to the DAB or to arbitration, the members may wish to view evidence of the Contractor's assumptions, query the authors and query why this evidence was not provided to the Engineer at an earlier date.

4.13   Rights of Way and Facilities

Occasionally it may happen that the Contractor requires other rights of access to the Site in addition to those provided by the Employer under the terms of the Contract. The Contractor has the duty to obtain such rights of way at his own risk and cost.

In addition, the Contractor may wish to occupy areas not within the Site and not otherwise within areas to be provided by the Employer under the terms of the Contract. Again, the Contractor has the duty to obtain use of these areas at his own risk and cost.

4.14   Avoidance of Interference

'*The Contractor may not interfere unnecessarily or improperly with the convenience of the public, access and use of footpaths*'. As a consequence the Contractor is obliged to negotiate and agree with the relevant authority or owner how any unavoidable interference shall be managed. The Engineer should be kept informed of proceedings. The Contractor under the terms of the Contract shall indemnify the Employer against all damages, losses and costs. This forms part of the Contractor's Third Party Insurance (refer to Sub-Clause 18.3).

4.15   Access Routes

In the preparation of the Tender, The Contractor has the obligation to satisfy himself '*as to the suitability and availability of access routes to the Site and other work areas*'.

Many public authorities have strict rules concerning the use by the Contractor of roads falling under their authority and the Contractor's requirements may have to be negotiated in some detail. The Contractor may be required to contribute to road-protection measures or maintenance costs.

Early clarification is needed since the estimated cost of any such measures has to be included in the Tender offer.

4.16   Transport of Goods

'*The Contractor is to give the Engineer not less than 21 days notice of the date of arrival of Plant and major items of Goods on Site*'. Further, the Contractor is responsible for all aspects of Goods arriving on Site.

It is assumed that the Contractor will have prepared a full schedule of the intended arrival date on site of his Plant and major items of Goods. These schedules could be periodically updated with arrival dates shown for presentation to the Engineer.

All Contractor's Plant and Goods are to be insured for their on-site value.

4.17   Contractor's Equipment

All Contractor's Equipment when brought on Site '*shall be deemed to be exclusively intended for the execution of the Works*'. Major items shall not be removed from Site without the permission of the Engineer.

Contractor's Equipment includes Subcontractor's Equipment and appropriate reference is to be included in the Subcontract Documents. It should be clarified if hire trucks and hire cars are excluded from this requirement.

4.18   Protection of Environment

The Contractor is required '*to take all reasonable steps to protect the environment (both on and off the Site) and to limit damage, nuisance and pollution*'. Increasingly, governments and local agencies have legal authority to ensure the protection of the environment by the Contractor and his subcontractors and suppliers. Specific requirements may include controlled disposal of inert waste of construction materials such as concrete, asphalt, rubble etc. Toxic materials such as waste oil and paint will require special disposal provisions. Domestic and office waste may be recyclable, otherwise permission to burn combustible waste may be required. Fees or charges may be imposed by the relevant authorities.

Should the Contractor provide living accommodation, the disposal of treated waste water and sewage is likely to be strictly controlled.

All these requirements have a cost implication to be evaluated by the Contractor for inclusion in the tender.

4.19   Electricity, Water and Gas

Other than provided in the Contract, the Contractor is *'responsible for the supply of the above services at his own risk and expense'*.

If Employer-provided services are already available at or near the site, the Contractor may be required to provide metering devices. Normally, if the Employer is to provide these services and the Site has a potentially high demand, it is necessary that the Parties liaise to ensure that the services are available, are of sufficient capacity and are not subject to shortages or other factors that could cause delays to the Works. This is particularly important if more than one contractor is taking supplies; peak requirements, particularly for the supply of electricity, may exceed the Employer's ability to supply.

4.20   Employer's Equipment and Free-Issue Material

It may be that the Employer has available equipment or materials which he wishes the Contractor to utilise on the Works. As a general rule, it is not compulsory for the Contractor to use the Employer's Equipment and Free-Issue Material. Frequently the potential use of these items is included by means of optional bill items in order to reduce the Tender Price if at all possible. Details, arrangements and prices of the Employer's Equipment and Free-Issue Material are to be given in the tender documentation. The Employer's Equipment and Free-Issue Material have to conform to the Specifications.

Whilst this sub-clause states that the Employer is responsible for the Employer's Equipment, the Contractor is strongly advised to inspect the Equipment very carefully, particularly since the Contract may contain wording making the Contractor responsible for the Equipment after handing over. It may be appropriate to make a full report including a photographic record of the condition of the Equipment no later than the date of handover. Self-evidently, these inspections should be made by suitably qualified members of the Contractor's staff. Even with such precautions, there is always the danger of latent defaults or defects in the Employer's Equipment after installation.

'The Employer shall supply free of charge the Free-Issue Material (if any) in accordance with the specification and shall at his own risk and cost provide those materials at the time and place specified in the Contract'. Nonetheless, it may be stated in the Particular Conditions that the Contractor shall collect the Free-Issue Material from a given location not necessarily within the Site.

The Contractor is required to visually inspect the Free-Issue Material and shall promptly give notice to the Engineer of any shortages, defects or default. The Employer is required to immediately rectify the shortages, defect or default.

The Contractor's obligations to safeguard the Free-Issue Material after handover '*shall not relieve the Employer of his liability for any shortage, defect or default not apparent from a visual inspection*'.

The Contractor should ensure that he has insurances to cover his liabilities for safeguarding the Employer's Equipment.

4.21   Progress Reports

It has long been a requirement of most contracts that the Contractor prepares monthly progress reports for submittal to the Engineer.

By this sub-clause FIDIC has now introduced formality and structure to this reporting system.

Of particular importance to the Contractor is the cross-reference contained in Sub-Clause 14.3, wherein it is stated that an Application for Interim Payment Certificates by the Contractor shall (as part of the supporting documentation) include a progress report for the same period to which the Interim Payment Application refers. Thus, any delay in providing the progress report may damage the Contractor's interests. The Contractor therefore should ensure that the progress report is efficiently prepared and submitted in time.

Sub-Clause 4.21 identifies eight topics to be addressed in the progress report although it is quite possible that other topics may have to be added to meet the special features of individual projects.

It is stated that each report shall cover the following topics:

(a) '*Charts and detailed description of progress*' (including Subcontractors and Nominated Subcontractors). This will centre on the Contractor's progress measured against programmes (see also (h) below)
(b) Photographs
(c) The status of the manufacture of the main items of Plant and Materials
(d) Records of Contractor's Personnel and Equipment (Sub-Clause 6.10)
(e) '*Copies of quality assurance documents, test results and certificates of Materials*'. It may be more convenient to supply bulk documents under separate cover and include only summaries in the report.
(f) '*List of notices under Sub-Clause 2.5 (Employer) and notices under Sub-Clause 20.1 (Contractor)*'
(g) '*Safety Statistics*'
(h) '*Comparisons of actual vs. planned progress*'. Details of delay events and measures to be taken to overcome the delay
(i) Other

The Contractor may seek to take the opportunity to highlight other topics that are not included in the above.

Owing to the limited time window available for the collection of data and the compilation of reports, it is important that the Contractor uses proforma model documents to the maximum extent possible.

In this respect it is recommended that the Contractor presents his proposals for the format and content of the reports to the Engineer for discussion at an early stage of the Contract in order that progress reports are prepared in an acceptable manner from the outset.

The Contractor's Representative will need to delegate responsibility for the preparation of various elements of the reports to the appropriate members of his staff. Further, he will need to nominate a suitable person to collate, edit and complete the final preparation of the progress reports. Finally, he should be willing to use his full authority to ensure that the nominated staff complete their given tasks according to a pre-set time schedule.

The Contractor is required to present progress reports until he has completed all work known to be outstanding at the completion date stated in the Taking Over Certificate.

4.22   Security of Site

This clause requires that the Contractor keeps unauthorised persons off the Site. Authorised persons are limited to the Contractor's Personnel and any other personnel notified to the Contractor by the Employer or the Engineer including authorised personnel of the Employer's other contractors on the Site (if any).

In addition, although not stated in this sub-clause, the Contractor necessarily may need to safeguard his assets both on or off Site including office and accommodation areas. There is no specific statement that the Contractor has to safeguard the assets of the Employer or Engineer (or their staff) on Site. Nonetheless, good security is of benefit to the Site and the companies employed there, and a pragmatic approach to the security of all is recommended.

There may also be insurance issues to be considered.

4.23   Contractor's Operations on Site

The Contractor is required to '*confine his operations to the Site and any additional work areas*' that may be agreed. This requirement extends to the Contractor's Equipment and Personnel. The Contractor is required to keep the Site free from obstructions and remove from Site any rubbish and other unwanted items. Upon the issue of a Taking Over Certificate, '*the Contractor is required to leave the Site and the Works in clean safe condition*'. Approved dump areas operated according to the laws of the country may be required. The Contractor may incur charges as a consequence. Cross-reference should also be made to Sub-Clause 4.18 'Protection of the Environment'.

4.24   Fossils

Although headed 'Fossils', this sub-clause also refers to coins, articles of value or antiquity and other items of geological or archaeological interest. Upon discovering any of the above, '*The Contractor shall give notice*' (recommended verbal notice followed by written notice) '*to the Engineer*', copy to the Employer.

The Engineer shall give instructions to the Contractor as to how to proceed with the Works which would include any necessary measures.

Should the Contractor consider that he will be delayed or otherwise incur additional costs, he should promptly give written notice of claim with reference to this sub-clause and Sub-Clause 20.1.

The FIDIC Guide comments that '*this sub-clause makes no reference to the finding of fossils having to be unforeseeable because the Contract should specify the procedure in respect of foreseeable findings.*'

The Contractor should be alert to any requirements of the local law.

Chapter 1

Clause 5 Nominated Subcontractors

This clause of the contract is prefaced in the FIDIC Guide with some notes of caution. Although these advisory notes are primarily directed towards the Employer and the Engineer, they are also of interest to Contractors as they provide an insight into the reasoning behind the engagement of nominated Subcontractors for the Works:

(i)   'If there are restrictions relating to the manufacture of certain items of Plant or Materials, the specification may refer to the named manufacturer without making him a nominated Subcontractor.'

(ii) If the Employer requires that 'a part of the Works is executed by a specialist company, the Specification may include a list of acceptable Subcontractors' inviting the Contractor to make his own choice. 'The selected Subcontractor would not then be a nominated Subcontractor.'

(iii) Should the Employer wish to become significantly involved in design and execution using a specialist company, a separate contract may be preferable.

The FIDIC Contract does not specifically state who will prepare the sub-contract document, but the following Clause 5.2 is so written that it is the obligation of the Employer to draw up the subcontract document. This also implies that it is the duty of the Employer to negotiate the terms of the Subcontract with the prospective Subcontractor. The Contractor does not have to accept any greater risk than the risk already contained within the Contract, particularly with respect to key issues such as insurances and payment conditions. Unless specifically stated in the Contract, the Contractor is under no obligation to provide other services such as vehicles, accommodation, materials, use of Contractor services, notably workshop services. The percentage for the Contractor's overheads and profit does not include the cost of these additional services if available. It is preferable that the Subcontractor shall include these costs within his subcontract price and pay the Contractor for any consumption on an 'as and when' basis provided always that the Contractor is able and willing to provide those additional services.

As a consequence of the above, there is potentially a considerable benefit to both Parties should the Employer involve the Contractor at an early stage of his negotiations with prospective nominated Subcontractors in order that any additional requirements of the Subcontractors can be identified and quantified. In addition, this consultative process would provide opportunity for discussion on technical issues and the programming of the Subcontract Works.

The nominated Subcontractor will be required to provide the Contractor with a Performance Security and evidence of his insurances. Should the nominated Subcontractor be the beneficiary of an Advance Payment, an Advance Payment Guarantee will be required. These and similar matters need to be addressed in the preparation of the nominated subcontract.

5.1 Definition of 'Nominated Subcontractor'

'The term "nominated Subcontractor" means a Subcontractor:

(a) *who is stated in the Contract to be a nominated Subcontractor.'* In addition to technical information contained in the Contract, a Provisional Sum will have been included in the Bills of Quantities (cross-refer to Sub-Clause 13.5) or

(b) *'whom the Engineer instructs the Contractor to employ as a Subcontractor.'* For payment purposes, such instruction shall be referenced to Sub-Clause 13.3 'Variations' or Sub-Clause 13.6 'Daywork'.

5.2 Objection to Nomination

The Contractor has the right to object to the engagement of a nominated Subcontractor. He is required to give notice of his objection to the Engineer as soon as practical with reasoning for his objection. Reasons for objection could include:

- Concerns that the Subcontractor does not have the required expertise, experience, resources or financial strength
- Failure of the Employer to agree to indemnify the Contractor against negligence by the nominated Subcontractor
- The subcontract does not specify that the nominated Subcontractor will undertake the obligations and liabilities in such a manner and timing as will *'enable the Contractor to fulfil his own obligations and liabilities under the Contract'*
- *'The subcontract does not indemnify the Contractor against and from all obligations and liabilities arising under the Contract and from the consequences of any failure by the Subcontractor to meet his obligations and liabilities arising under the Subcontract.'*

5.3 Payments to Nominated Subcontractors

'The Contractor shall pay to the nominated Subcontractor the amounts which the Engineer certifies to be due in accordance with the subcontract.' The Contractor shall be paid the same amount plus a percentage for the Contractor's overheads and profit.

It is appropriate that the subcontract provides that the Contractor pays the Subcontractor within a fixed number of days from the date on which the Contractor receives payment under the Contract. The number of days is to be specifically stated in the Subcontract documents.

5.4 Evidence of Payments

Before issuing a Payment Certificate that includes an amount payable to a nominated Subcontractor, the Engineer may request evidence that previously certified amounts due under the Subcontract have been paid to the Subcontractor.

Any failure to make payment to nominated Subcontractors when due may entitle the Employer to make direct payment.

Especially on very large projects it is recommended that matters concerning the Contract that involve the Employer and the Engineer are separated from those matters solely concerning the Contractor and the nominated Subcontractor. Any claims or disputes between Contractor and the nominated Subcontractor that directly relate to the performance of the Contract have to be managed to conform to the requirements of the Contract. Claims and disputes that solely relate to the contractual relationship between the Contractor and the nominated Subcontractor have to be managed in accordance with the Subcontract, where there is greater scope for flexibility without the involvement of the Employer and the Engineer.

Similarly, payments due to the nominated Subcontractor under the terms of the Contract should preferably be managed separately from other domestic payment matters such as payment for any services provided. It is recommended that the Contractor ensures that formal interim payment certificates are issued to the nominated Subcontractor once the Contractor receives his own certification under the Contract. Any other payment due from Contractor to the nominated Subcontractor or vice versa should be dealt with separately as a simple commercial transaction in order that the content of the Interim Payment Certificates is not obscured.

Clause 6 Staff and Labour

6.1   Engagement of Staff and Labour

The Contractor is responsible for the engagement, payment, accommodation and transport of all staff and labour. The extent of the Contractor's obligations will depend on the location of the Works and local law regulation.

6.2   Rates of Wages and Conditions of Labour

'*The Contractor is required to pay wages and observe conditions of labour which are not lower than those established for trade and industry where the work is carried out.*' Frequently these wages and conditions of labour are established by law usually with the cooperation of trade unions or wage councils. Premiums may have to be paid for key workers or those with scarce skills. In preparation of his tender, the Contractor is required to take account of the wages and conditions prevalent at Base Date and additional payment may be due in accordance with Sub-Clauses 13.7 and 13.8.

6.3   Persons in Service of Employer

The Contractor shall not seek to employ staff or labour already engaged by the Employer.

6.4   Labour Laws

'*The Contractor is obliged to comply with all relevant labour laws* and *shall allow them all their legal rights*' which would include the right to form and join Trade Unions. '*The Contractor shall require his employees to obey all applicable laws with particular reference to safety at work*.' Such obligations can be addressed in letters of employment with each employee.

6.5   Working Hours

'*No work shall be carried out on the Site on locally recognised days of rest or outside the normal working hours stated in the Appendix to the Tender, unless:*

(a)   *otherwise stated in the Contract*
(b)   *the Engineer gives consent*
(c)   *the work is unavoidable for the protection of life, property or safety of the Works. The Contractor has to advise the Engineer in such instances.*'

There is a growing tendency for the Employer to state fixed working hours in the Contract which correspond to standard hours worked in government offices or commercial enterprises. These standard hours are often set in law or by agreement with the Trade Unions. Even so, an amount of overtime working is not prohibited.

Although it may not be stated in the Contract, it may be assumed that the Engineer's service agreement will similarly limit the work hours of his staff.

Should the Contractor request permission to work outside the stated hours, his request may be rejected or he may be required to pay the additional cost of overtime hours worked by the Engineer's staff. However, it is not the practice of employers to provide details of the overtime rates applicable to the Engineer's staff which would enable the Contractor to make a proper evaluation, so that an allowance could be made in the Tender. Further, whilst it is understandable that no one wishes to work unpaid overtime hours, paid overtime can be divisive and difficult to control.

The problem is highlighted when the Contractor's operations require a night shift, e.g. for quarry operations, transportation etc., in order to make best use of the Contractor's Plant and Equipment.

Summer work, most notably the placement of asphalt, may necessitate working extended hours to compensate for the loss of productivity in the winter months and other periods of adverse weather.

Should the Contractor consider it inevitable that overtime hours necessarily have to be worked during the performance of the Contract, the Engineer should be requested to clarify the intentions of the Employer as part of the tendering process. It is assumed that a policy of 'openness' by the Employer would also be to his benefit. This would enable the Contractor to correctly price his Tender offer with less likelihood of future disputes and more importantly it would improve the quality of the Contractor's planning with an important risk element properly evaluated.

6.6   Facilities for Staff and Labour

Unless stated elsewhere in the contract documents, the Contractor is required to provide accommodation and welfare facilities for his personnel. There are a number of possible scenarios. The Contractor may choose to provide on-site accommodation for the majority of his personnel, particularly if the site is in a remote location and the majority of his personnel are recruited from other countries or other regions of the host country. In contrast, in more developed countries, with plentiful supply of local labour, the Contractor may elect to accommodate his workforce either in their own homes or in rented property in locations convenient to the Site.

The Contractor may also be required to provide accommodation for the Employer's and Engineer's personnel.

Consideration has to be given to the provision of mess-halls, 'drying' rooms, sanitary facilities and similar for the total workforce. These may be specifically required by local laws and in any event the Trade Unions may have strong views in respect of these matters.

The provision of these facilities represents a significant cost to the Contractor and appropriate allowance has to be made in the tender offer.

6.7   Health and Safety

'*The Contractor is required at all times to take reasonable steps to maintain the health and safety of his personnel*', this basic requirement almost certainly being far more explicitly stated in local laws and regulations.

The Contractor is required to ensure '*that medical staff, first aid facilities, sick bay and ambulance services are available at all times at the site*'. The precise requirements will vary considerably from project to project, from location to location, from the size and complexity of the site operations and not least from the amount of support available from local hospitals and health services. Should a sizeable part of the Contractor's staff be expatriate in origin, evacuation plans to return injured or sick expatriates to their own country may also be required.

As a first step, it is necessary to meet with local medical professionals to ascertain what facilities are locally available and how they might be accessed by the Contractor. This will have an impact on decisions taken in respect of medical facilities and staff to be provided by the Contractor on Site.

It may be expected that the Engineer will require the Contractor to provide a detailed proposal to cover all medical aspects of health and safety.

Clause 6.7 further requires the Contractor to make all necessary welfare arrangements and to be responsible for hygiene.

Welfare arrangements in this context would include messing and feeding arrangements, the provision of drying rooms and similar. Hygiene requirements would include adequate toilet and washing facilities and a general regard for the preventative measures against disease and unhealthy work practices.

The Contractor is required '*to appoint an accident prevention officer at the Site, responsible for maintaining safety and protection against accidents.*' The person shall be required to be qualified for this work and to be given authority to issue instructions and take protective measures.

These general requirements can be expected to be amplified in the Contract and will be subject to the relevant laws of the country.

Most major contractors will have available formal Health and Safety Manuals. The accident-prevention officer will need to supplement these manuals to conform with the requirements of the Contract and the local law. Parts of the safety manuals may require translation into the local language(s). Period reporting is required and will form part of the Progress Report described in Sub-Clause 4.21.

6.8   Contractor's Superintendence

In addition to the Contractor's Representative described in Sub-Clause 4.3, the Contractor is required to provide all necessary supervision for the full performance of the Contract. The superintendents are required to have the necessary experience and skills. A sufficient number are required to have adequate knowledge of the language of the Contract. It is implied that translators will also be required.

6.9   Contractor's Personnel

'*The Contractor's Personnel are to be appropriately qualified, skilled and experienced in their respective trades or occupations.*' The Engineer has the right to order the removal from Site of any person who fails in a number of ways to be suitable for employment on Site. This does not imply that the employment of the unsuitable personnel is automatically to be terminated by the Contractor. Local laws may provide for an appeals procedure against unfair dismissal.

6.10   Records of Contractor's Personnel and Equipment

At monthly intervals (refer to Sub-Clause 4.21) the Contractor is required to produce a report to the Engineer detailing the numbers and classifications of the Contractor's Personnel and a detailed listing of the Contractor's Equipment on site.

6.11   Disorderly Conduct

The Contractor has the duty to '*prevent disorderly conduct amongst and by the Contractor's Personnel and to preserve peace on Site.*'

Clause 7 Plant, Materials and Workmanship

7.1   Manner of Execution

'*The Contractor shall carry out the manufacture of Plant, the production and manufacture of Materials and all other execution of the Works*

(a)   *in the manner (if any) specified in the Contract*
(b)   *in a proper workmanlike and careful manner … with recognised good practice*
and
(c)   *with properly equipped facilities and non-hazardous Materials.*'

The FIDIC guide explains: '*Many manufacturing processes are hazardous, but do not result in "hazardous" materials. Materials must not require the use of hazardous Site procedures for them to "form … part of the Permanent Works" on the Site. Materials shall not be hazardous thereafter. The Engineer is not empowered to relax this provision of Contract.*'

7.2   Samples

The Contractor is required '*to submit the following samples and relevant information to the Engineer for consent prior to using the Materials in or for the Works:*

(a)   *Manufacturer's standard samples of Materials and samples specified in the Contract, all at the Contractor's cost*'. The Contractor should ensure that any costs are passed on to the manufacturer within his price quotation.
(b)   '*Additional samples ordered by the Engineer as a Variation*'.

7.3   Inspection

'*The Employer's Personnel shall have full access to all parts of the Site and all places where natural Materials are being obtained*' (borrow areas, quarries etc. which may be off-Site). Additionally, the Engineer is entitled to inspect, test etc. materials and workmanship during production, manufacture and construction (at the Site and elsewhere).

'*He is authorised to check the manufacture of Plant whether on or off Site. The Contractor shall give notice to the Engineer when any work is ready and before it is covered up*' (and/or dispatched).

Special provisions may apply for major items of Plant manufactured off-Site, particularly if the place of manufacture is in another country. The Employer may nominate an agency to carry out inspections and tests on his behalf in such circumstances. Unless stated otherwise in the Contract, the Employer is responsible for his own costs.

In preparing his tender offer, the Contractor should clarify who is responsible to meet the costs of any inspection or testing and make appropriate provision in his tender.

7.4   Testing

The Contractor is required to provide everything necessary for the performance of specified tests including suitably qualified personnel.

'*The Contractor shall agree with the Engineer the time and place for the specified testing.*' If the Engineer does not attend at the agreed time and place, the Contractor may continue with the testing. If the Engineer causes delay to the Works, the Contractor is entitled to claim an extension of time and reimbursement of any additional costs incurred. The Claim has to be referenced to Sub-Clause 20.1.

After completion of the test programme, the Contractor shall promptly forward certified reports of the tests to the Engineer. '*When the specified tests have passed the requirements of the Contract, the Engineer shall endorse the Contractor's test certificate.*' It is to be noted that Sub-Clause 4.21(c) also refers to submittal of data in respect of testing of Plant and Materials.

Less experienced contractors not infrequently assume that because a successful inspection or test has taken place the work is approved and therefore is not subject to further scrutiny. Sub-Clause 11.9 makes it clear that the Works are not finally approved until the issue of the Completion Certificate. This proviso enables the Engineer to review any aspect of testing at any stage of the execution of the Works.

7.5   Rejection

'*If as a result of inspection or testing any Plant, Materials or workmanship is found to be defective or otherwise not in accordance with the Contract, the Engineer may issue a rejection notice stating the reasons for the rejection and the Contractor shall make good the defect.*'

If re-testing is necessary and the Employer incurs additional costs, the Employer is entitled to claim reimbursement in accordance with the provisions of Sub-Clause 2.5.

7.6   Remedial Work

'*Notwithstanding any previous test or certification, the Engineer may instruct the Contractor to:*'

(a) remove, replace and re-execute '*any work not in accordance with the Contract*
(b) *execute any work which is urgently required for the safety of the Works.*'

If the Contractor fails to comply, the Employer may engage others to carry out the work and, subject to the provisions of Sub-Clause 2.5, the Contractor is required to pay all costs of the Engineer arising from this failure.

7.7   **Ownership of Plant and Materials**

'*Each item of Plant and Materials shall, to the extent consistent with the laws of the country, become the property of the Employer free from liens and encumbrances*

(a)   *when it is delivered to site*

(b)   *when the Contractor is entitled to payment of the value of the Plant and Materials under Sub-Clause 8.10 (Payment for Plant and Materials in Event of Suspension)*'

It may be important to establish the legal ownership of Plant and Materials, particularly in the event of bankruptcy/liquidation of the person who is in possession of them. For example, some plant may be owned by Subcontractors, or be the subject of hire agreement or hire-purchase agreement. This is a complex topic. Local law will prevail and legal advice would be necessary to protect the rights of the Contractor and the Subcontractors and creditors.

Reference may be also made to Sub-Clauses 14.3(a) and 14.5, which provide for interim payments to be made to the Contractor for Plant and Materials intended for the Works and delivered to site – all subject to specified conditions.

7.8   **Royalties**

'*Unless otherwise stated in the Specification, the Contractor shall pay all royalties and rents and other payments for:*

■ *natural Materials obtained from outside the Site.*' In many countries a licence is required before natural material is taken from borrow areas, quarries, river beds and similar. For government-owned land, royalties are fixed by decree. Extraction from private land may also be subject to payment of royalties to government authorities in addition to payments to the owner of the land. In some locations those charges can be significant and they should be quantified and the total cost included in the Tender Price.

■ Disposal of waste, surplus or otherwise unsuitable materials, is frequently subjected to a tax regime. Disposal areas are increasingly strictly controlled and haul distances to those disposal areas may be significant. Abnormal pollutants such as chemicals, asbestos, oils etc. may require special precautions.

■ Finally, there may be environmental requirements imposed by the authorities (cross-refer to Sub-Clause 4.18 'Protection of Environment').

The full cost of all the above has to be evaluated and included in the tender offer.

Clause 8 Commencement, Delays and Suspension

8.1   Commencement of Work

'*The Engineer shall give the Contractor 7 days notice of the Commencement Date.*' Commencement Date is the date on which the Time for Completion commences.

'*The Commencement Date shall be within 42 days after the Contractor receives the Letter of Acceptance. If there is no letter of acceptance, the expression "Letter of Acceptance" means the Contract Agreement and the date of issuing the Letter of Acceptance means the date of signing the Contract Agreement*' (refer to definition under Sub-Clause 1.1.1.3).

Within the provided period of 42 days the Employer will doubtlessly be completing his own arrangements relating to the Commencement of Work, the most significant of which from the Contractor's point of view will be the so-called handover of Site (refer to Sub-Clause 2.1 'Right of Access to the Site').

Sub-Clause 2.1 'Right of Access to Site', including handover of site, is not specifically linked to Sub-Clause 8.1 'Commencement of Work'. The Appendix to Tender may contain data confirming that Access to Site will take place at a date after the Commencement Date. In such case the Contractor will be limited to off-Site preparatory activities.

8.2   Time for Completion

This sub-clause confirms the obligation of the Contractor to complete the whole of the Works, and each section (if any), within the Time for Completion measured from the Commencement Date. Conventionally, the Time for Completion is stated in the Appendix to Tender (refer to discussion under Sub-Clause 1.5).

8.3   Programme

The Employer may have provided an outline programme with the Tender Documents in order to demonstrate to the Contractor and others the feasibility of constructing the Works within the Time for Completion given in the Tender Documents. Alternatively, the Contractor may be required to provide his own outline programme in sufficient detail to demonstrate compliance with the requirements of the Tender Documents. From the Employer's viewpoint the Contractor's outline programme would also demonstrate the Contractor's understanding of the work to be undertaken.

It is possible that the tender programme, whether produced by the Employer or the Contractor, will be modified as a consequence of any post-tender meetings. Consequently, it is likely, but by no means certain, that an outline programme of works will be included in the Contract Documents. This programme has many important consequences. For example, the date(s) by which the Employer is required to give the Contractor access to Site should be readily identifiable.

This sub-clause requires that '*each programme shall include*

- *the order in which the Contractor intends to carry out the Work including the anticipated timing of each stage*' of the various components of the Works
- the anticipated timing for any work by nominated Subcontractors
- '*the sequence and timing of any inspection and testing*' (this is particularly applied to significant items of Equipment)
- '*a general description of methods to be employed in the execution of the Works.*' It may be assumed that the word 'general' recognises that more time will be required to produce fully detailed method statements
- identification of key resources to be employed

Ideally, it would be hoped that the general basis for the Programme has already been developed prior to the Commencement Date. The Contractor has only 28 days after the Commencement Date to submit the Programme to the Engineer. This is a relatively short period in which to produce a fully detailed programme. This period is a very active period for the Contractor, as he is likely to be involved in the many more essential activities that are part of the initial establishment on Site.

The Programme is important not only for the planning and control of the execution of the Works; it is also the base document by which any request for Extension of Time will be evaluated. It is important that the task of producing the Programme is given to the member(s) of the Contractor's staff with the appropriate experience and competence. The task should not be left to junior staff with the intention of simply doing the minimum to satisfy the requirements of the Contract.

The Engineer has 21 days in which to give notice to the Contractor of any objection he may have to the Contractor's submission. If the Engineer does not object, then it may be assumed that the Programme is accepted and can be used for the planning and execution of the Works.

Sub-Clause 8.3 continues by requiring the Contractor '*to give notice to the Engineer of events or circumstances*' affecting, or which might in the future affect, the planned progress of the Works and cause additional cost. The events or circumstances that entitle the Contractor to an extension of the Time for Completion are spread through various clauses and sub-clauses of the Contract. Consequently, any request for an Extension of Time from the Contractor requires a reference to the appropriate clause or sub-clause giving rise to the entitlement.

Assuming that the Contractor presents his claim in accordance with the provisions of Sub-Clause 20.1, the Engineer has a further fixed time limit in which to respond.

Various scenarios may then arise:

(a) The Engineer may concur with the Contractor's request and award an extension to the Time for Completion. The Programme will be modified accordingly.

(b) The Engineer may disagree with the Contractor's request. The Programme will not be modified. The Contractor is entitled to refer his claim to the next level of the dispute-resolution procedure but must continue with the Works at the contracted rate.

(c) The Engineer may not give a decision, or a decision may be given late, possibly because of restrictions imposed by the Employer. Many Employers find it very difficult to deal with requests for extensions of time separately from any financial consequences. Not infrequently a Contract can enter a contractual 'limbo', which can cause considerable difficulties both for the Engineer and the Contractor.

However, this sub-clause does contain the additional proviso whereby the Engineer can give notice to the Contractor that the progress of the Works is failing to comply with the requirements of the Contract and require the Contractor to submit a revised programme and/or proposals describing how the Contractor intends to recover any programme delay. Given the circumstances described in paragraph (c) above, the Contractor is obliged to react. At all times the Contractor has to comply with the Engineer's instructions validly given under the Contract.

By employing more resources, revised methods of working and extended hours, it may be feasible for the Contractor to make good lost time. Self-evidently, additional costs will arise in respect of which the Contractor is entitled to make a formal claim in accordance with the requirements of Sub-Clause 20.1. Good record-keeping is essential.

Should the delay be of such magnitude that cannot be recovered, the resultant delay to the Completion Date would leave the Contractor exposed to the imposition of Delay Damages or, in an extreme situation, to Termination by the Employer.

A continuing failure of the Engineer to deal expeditiously with the Contractor's requests for Extensions of Time for Completion can damage the interests of the Employer. Equally, the failure or unwillingness of the Contractor to recognise his own failings and take remedial action can damage his interests.

A combination of failings by both Parties, as described above, can have serious consequences for the overall management of the contract.

It frequently happens that the Contractor cannot complete by the Time for Completion and presents a revised programme showing his best expectations. He considers that he is entitled to Extensions of Time for all or part of the delay and has made appropriate applications to the Engineer.

The Engineer for whatever reasons may not have dealt promptly with the Contractor's requests, and may either reject the revised programme and require revisions which could be unrealistic, or he may choose to allow the Contractor to continue with the proposed revised programme at the Contractor's risk with the intention of dealing with the Contractor's claim only once, when the Works are already the subject of a Taking Over Certificate.

Once the Taking Over Certificate is issued, it is convenient for the Employer and Engineer to provide the Contractor with an Extension of Time for Completion of just sufficient duration conforming to the effective date of the Taking Over Certificate. Regrettably, this is usually tied to an unfavourable level of settlement of the outstanding claims of the Contractor. Such offers are without contractual or economic logic and are often more linked to the availability of Employer funding. To prevent himself being unduly disadvantaged, the Contractor is strongly advised to faithfully adhere to the requirements of the Contract by giving notice in good time and adhering strictly to the dispute-resolution procedures given in the Contract and not being deflected by any failings of others. Nonetheless, it is equally important that the Contractor recognises his own failings and takes remedial action at the earliest opportunity.

The evaluation of time delays to the Works can be both tedious and time-consuming and frequently lead to an unsatisfactory outcome. Simple delays, where the critical path to completion is very evident, may be readily solved by the Parties, particularly if their relationship is positive and supportive.

In contrast, in contracts where a number of updated programmes have been produced during the period of execution, the critical path to completion can become obscured or (where tasks have been affected by resource limitations) entitlements to Extensions of Time for Completion can become very difficult to resolve.

There are a number of computer-driven techniques available to analyse such complex delays to the level as would be suitable for presentation to a DAB or Arbitration Board.

However, the basis for all such analysis is derived from the quality and detail of the original programme and an accurate recording of all the events and circumstances that have affected, or will affect, the performance of the Contract.

By definition, claims for Extensions of Time for Completion are Contractor Claims. The Engineer has no obligation to help the Contractor in this task. Self-evidently, the Contractor cannot record everything that happens on the Site in microscopic detail, particularly for smaller projects.

It is important that the Contractor's staff concerned with claim issues develop a clear strategy for dealing with both physical and administrative requirements for data collection in order to prepare and develop Claims. It is not appropriate to rely on data to be gathered in a random manner at a later date when key staff may have already left the Site. The use of standard reporting forms is recommended (refer to Appendix F).

8.4   Extension of Time for Completion

The sub-clause identifies the circumstances that would entitle the Contractor to claim an Extension of Time for Completion.

The following causes are listed:

(a) '*Variations or a substantial change in the quantity of the work included in the Contract*'
(b) '*A cause of delay identified under a Sub-Clause of these Conditions*'
(c) '*Exceptionally adverse climatic conditions*'

(d)   '*Unforeseeable shortages in the availability of personnel or goods caused by epidemic or government actions*'

(e)   '*Delays impediment or prevention caused by or attributable to the Employer, the Employer's Personnel or the Employer's other contractors on site.*'

The Contractor is required to give notice to the Engineer in accordance with Sub-Clause 20.1. The Engineer is empowered to review previous determinations, but shall not decrease the extension of time previously granted.

8.5   Delay Caused by Authorities

Delays caused by authorities (and service providers) are frequently the source of delays and irritation. It is not uncommon for authorities, because they are not part of the Contract, to have little interest in completing their statutory obligations as expeditiously as desired. In many instances due to under-funding and shortages of materials available to the authority and other providers, the Contractor is frequently required to physically intervene to assist the authority.

To obtain an Extension of Time for Completion and additional payment, the following criteria apply:

(a)   '*The Contractor has to have diligently followed the procedures laid down by the relevant legally constituted public authorities in the country.*' It is required that the Contractor obtain information concerning the procedures to be followed at the tender stage and certainly no later than the Commencement Date.

(b)   '*The authorities delay or disrupt the Contractor's Work.*' Ideally, the Employer will have advised the authorities of the detail and programming of the Works.

(c)   '*The delay or disruption was unforeseeable.*' By following the procedures of the authorities and by supporting the Employer to keep the authorities advised of the detail and programming of the Works, it is easier to demonstrate unforeseeability.

8.6   Rate of Progress

If the '*actual progress is too slow to complete within the Time for Completion and/or progress has fallen (or will fall) behind the current programme* (refer to Sub-Clause 8.3) *other than as a result of a cause listed in Sub-Clause 8.4, then the Engineer may instruct the Contractor to submit a revised programme* (refer to commentary in Sub-Clause 8.3) *complete with a supporting report.*'

Any additional costs are to the account of the Contractor, unless the Engineer notifies otherwise (refer, for example, to Sub-Clause 13.2 'Acceleration to overcome excusable delay'.

The Contractor should treat any notice delivered by the Engineer under this sub-clause very seriously. To ignore a notice given under this sub-clause might – in an extreme situation – lead to Termination by the Employer – Sub-Clause 15.2(c)(ii) refers.

8.7   Delay Damages

'*If the Contractor fails to comply with Sub-Clause 8.2 "Time for Completion", the Contractor shall pay Delay Damages to the Employer for this default. The amount and limit for Delay Damages shall be as stated in the Appendix to Tender.*'

'*These Delay Damages shall be the only damages due from the Contractor as a consequence of the default (excepting in the event of Termination by the Employer Sub-Clause 15.2).*' The Employer cannot claim his actual costs, but equally does not have to demonstrate his actual loss.

The FIDIC Guide explains that '*the Contractor cannot prevent the imposition of Delay Damages by submitting claims for extension of time. However, the Employer may lose his entitlement to claim delay damages if he prevents extensions of time being agreed or determined in accordance with Sub-Clause 20.1*' (cross-refer to possible restrictions placed on the authority of the Engineer under Sub-Clause 3.1).

Should he wish to claim Delay Damages, the Employer is required to present a documented claim to the Engineer, as provided for in Sub-Clause 2.5. The Engineer is required to formally review the claim in accordance with the provisions of Sub-Clause 3.5. It should be noted that Sub-Clause 3.5 requires the Engineer to consult with each Party before making a 'fair determination'. This procedure would give the Contractor the possibility to object should the Engineer be blocked by the Employer from making a determination in respect of the Contractor's existing claims for extensions of time.

8.8   Suspension of Work

This sub-clause gives the Engineer the authority to suspend all or part of the Works.

During the execution of the Works, circumstances may arise that result in the Works having to be suspended. The causes of the suspension can be divided into four categories:

(a)   Suspension necessary to meet the additional or changed requirements of the Employer. Examples could include the need for a major change in design, political considerations, financial limitations etc.

(b)   Suspension as a consequence of improper practices by the Contractor or his subcontractors. For example, safety concerns or the aftermath of an accident may result in a suspension ordered by the Engineer or a government authority.

(c)   Suspension resulting from an event for which neither Party is responsible. These causes are addressed in detail in Clause 19 'Force Majeure', which provides details of the Contractor's obligations and entitlements.

Chapter 1

(d)   Suspension arising from natural causes that are not force majeure. A major flood may automatically suspend the progress of Works.

The expectation is that the Engineer would instruct a suspension of work in respect of category (a) and possibly category (b) above. Self-evidently, there is no value in the Engineer issuing a formal suspension order in respect of categories (c) and (d).

Following receipt of a suspension instruction, the Contractor has a general duty *'to protect store and secure the Works.'*

8.9   Consequences of Suspension

For all events causing a Suspension of the Works, the Contractor must keep detailed records of all his activities and costs, since for the majority of causes the Contractor will be entitled to claim reimbursement from the Employer or his insurers.

It is particularly important that detailed records be maintained of idle resources. A lengthy suspension may require a rundown of manpower. The consequences should be discussed with the Employer and Engineer before their implementation.

'This Sub-Clause states that if the Contractor suffers delay or incurs cost from complying with the Engineer's instructions, he shall give notice to the Engineer and shall be entitled' (subject to compliance with Sub-Clause 20.1) to an extension of time (refer to Sub-Clause 8.4) and to payment of his costs. It is to be noted that this entitlement is conditional on the Engineer issuing instructions. Since it is unlikely that a Contractor would unilaterally suspend the Works for a category (a) cause listed in the above commentary for Sub-Clause 8.8, the Engineer would be obligated to issue an appropriate instruction.

The sub-clause concludes by stating that *'the Contractor shall not be entitled to an extension of time or payment of the cost incurred in making good faulty work or for any failure to protect store or secure in accordance with Sub-Clause 8.8.'*

8.10   Payment for Plant and Materials in Event of Suspension

'For a suspension which is not due to any failure on the part of the Contractor he is entitled to payment for any suspended Plant and Materials 28 days after the date of suspension if he takes necessary actions to make the Plant and Materials the property of the Employer.'

Inevitably, this process would have to be discussed and formalised with the Employer. The process is optional for the Contractor and may be varied should the cause of the suspension be related to financial issues. Payment of any entitlement would be under Clause 14 'Contract Price and Payment'.

8.11   Prolonged Suspension

'If the suspension under Sub-Clause 8.8 has continued for more than 84 days, the Contractor may request the Engineer for permission to proceed.

If the Engineer does not give permission within a further period of 28 days, the Contractor may, by giving notice to the Engineer, treat the suspension as an omission under Clause 13 "Variation and Adjustments". If the suspension affects the whole of the Works, the Contractor may give notice of termination under Sub-Clause 16.2.'

In an extreme situation a period of 112 days could elapse before the Contractor is advised whether the Works are to continue or if the period of suspension is to be extended by agreement or if the Works are to be terminated. The Contractor is placed at considerable commercial risk by any suspension and the uncertainty arising from an extended suspension amplifies those risks.

It is important for the Contractor to maintain close contact with the Employer and the Engineer in order to obtain an agreement concerning the future of the Contractor's resources both on and off Site. Good record-keeping by the Contractor is essential to support any claims subsequently presented by him.

8.12   Resumption of Work

'After the permission or instruction to proceed is given, the Contractor and the Engineer shall jointly examine the Works and the Plant and Materials affected by the suspension. The Contractor shall make good any deterioration or defect which has occurred during the suspension and is entitled to claim his costs under Sub-Clause 8.9 "Consequences of Suspension".'

It is quite possible that the suspension may have disrupted the Contractor's activities in other ways. Personnel may have left the Site and have to be recalled or new personnel recruited. It is very likely that some time will elapse before the Contractor reaches the productivity levels obtained before the suspension.

Any submittal made under Sub-Clause 8.9 should include any cost of disruption and requests for Extension of Time should include for any effective time loss due to the disruption.

Clause 9 Tests on Completion

9.1   Contractor's Obligations

The term Tests on Completion' is defined in Sub-Clause 1.1.3.4 as '*the tests which are specified in the Contract or agreed by both Parties or instructed as a Variation ... which are to be carried out before the Works or a Section are taken over by the Employer*'.

The great majority of tests will be performed as the Works proceed, but certain types of testing can only be performed when the Works are nearing completion. An example would be full-load tests on electrical systems. This sub-clause covers the possibility that certain specified tests must be completed before the Works can be taken over by the Employer. The tests may require an input from the Employer or service providers. Further, it is possible that some tests have to be satisfactorily performed to comply with the requirements and the attendance of the local authorities or service providers. Security equipment may also require testing to be completed before Taking Over.

The Taking Over of the Works described in Sub-Clause 10.1 allows for the possible existence of '*minor outstanding works and defects ...*' at the date of Taking Over that are to be completed in the Defects Liability Period. In some countries '*minor*' is strictly interpreted so that the amount of outstanding work is very minor indeed.

It is important that the Contractor ascertains the precise level of completion, including the extent of Tests on Completion, required for Taking Over by the Employer well in advance of the projected date of Taking Over.

This sub-clause requires the Contractor to give the Engineer not less than 21 days' notice of dates for the performance of Tests on Completion.

9.2   Delayed Tests

Should Tests on Completion be delayed by the Employer (refer to Sub-Clause 7.4, 5th paragraph, and Sub-Clause10.3), the Contractor is entitled to claim an extension of time and additional costs.

Alternatively, should the Contractor fail to carry out Tests on Completion, the Engineer may give notice to the Contractor to carry out the tests within a period of 21 days, otherwise the Employer's personnel may proceed with the tests at the risk and cost of the Contractor. In practice the Employer's personnel may be reluctant to unilaterally perform Tests on Completion, particularly if they are not familiar with the subject of the tests.

9.3   Re-testing

The Contractor is required to repeat any failed Tests on Completion. Any remedial works undertaken may affect other Tests on Completion.

9.4   Failure to Pass Tests on Completion

In the event of continued failure to satisfactorily complete the Tests on Completion, the Engineer may order further repeat testing (assumed to take place after checking and remedial work by the Contractor). If the continued failure to complete the Tests on Completion prevails, the Employer has available the remedies provided for in Sub-Clause 11.4(c). Alternatively, the Employer may authorise the Engineer to issue the Taking Over Certificate which carries the implication that the reasons for the failure to satisfactorily complete the Tests on Completion do not damage the Employer's interests.

Clause 10 Employer's Taking Over

10.1   Taking Over of the Works and Sections

The Works (or section) shall be taken over by the Employer when the Works have been completed in accordance with the Contract, including the passing of Tests on Completion (refer to Clause 9) with the exception of minor outstanding works and defects discussed below.

The issue of a formal Taking Over Certificate signifies that the Works (or section) have been taken over.

The Contractor is obliged to apply by notice to the Engineer, copied to the Employer, for a Taking Over Certificate not earlier than 14 days before the Works (or section) will – in the Contractor's opinion – be complete and ready for taking over.

'*The Engineer shall within 28 days after receiving the Contractor's application*

(a) *issue a Taking Over Certificate stating the date on which the Works (or section) were completed in accordance with the Contract, except for any minor outstanding work and defects which will not substantially affect the use of the Works (or section) for their intended purpose or*

(b) *reject the application giving reasons and specifying the work required to be done by the Contractor to enable the Taking Over Certificate to be issued.*'

Having completed those works which are identified in (a) above, the Contractor shall re-apply for the issue of the Taking Over Certificate in the same manner as before. This has the disadvantage that a further 42 days are lost until a new application can be actioned.

Consequently, as the anticipated date for Taking Over draws nearer, it is recommended that the Contractor maintains an increasingly detailed dialogue with the Engineer in order to continuously review the status of the Works, thereby establishing the extent of the Works yet to be completed. Such a dialogue would greatly facilitate the Taking Over process. However, it is usual for the Particular Conditions of Contract to be amended, preventing the Engineer from issuing a Taking Over Certificate without the agreement of the Employer (and, if appropriate, the end user of the Works).

In some countries (e.g. Romania, Bulgaria) there are statutory authorities who control the Taking Over process and the taking into use of the Works, all in accordance with the local law, thus circumventing the provisions of a FIDIC-based contract. Very often the bureaucratic nature of committees appointed by the authorities to oversee the Taking Over process in accordance with local law can be very tedious and time-consuming, leading to the Taking Over Certificate being issued later than might be the case under the Engineer-controlled Taking Over procedure inherent in a FIDIC-based contract. This situation could in theory leave the Contractor, possibly unfairly, exposed to the imposition of Delay Damages (Sub-Clause 8.7).

The Contractor, preferably in cooperation with the Engineer, who may also not be familiar with local procedures, should seek authoritative guidance at an early stage of the execution of the Contract.

Sub-Clause 10.1 continues by stating that if the Engineer fails to issue the Taking Over Certificate or fails to reject the Contractor's application within the stated period of 28 days, and if the Works are indeed substantially completed in accordance with the Contract, the Taking Over Certificate shall be deemed to have been issued on the last day of that period. It seems inevitable that the Employer will insist on the Engineer rejecting the Contractor's application without due cause or with improper reasoning rather than allow a Taking Over to take place by default. Additionally, the provisions of local law as described earlier may make such a Taking Over procedure illegal.

The Contractor should be very wary that he does not find himself trapped in a situation where a delay can be engineered between the Employer, the end user and the authorities, preventing the rightful use of the Taking Over Certificate, in order to meet the convenience of the Employer rather than complying with the stated intentions of the Contract. The Engineer may find his authority undermined in these circumstances. It further leaves the Contractor in a difficult position because it is not possible to estimate the time to be allowed in the programme for completion of this activity.

The Employer has no right to use the Works if the Contractor has failed to complete them in accordance with the Contract except after Termination.

10.2   Taking Over of Parts of the Works

'The Engineer may, at the sole discretion of the Employer issue a Taking Over Certificate for any part of the Permanent Works.'

Should the Employer require access to (and possibly operate) parts of the Works prior to the issue of a Taking Over Certificate, then such requirement either has to be stated in the Contract or a separate agreement made between the Parties.

Whilst the Employer and Contractor may make a supplementary agreement permitting the Employer to occupy parts of the Works without formal Taking Over, in practice this should be used sparingly. Not only are there plenty of opportunities for disputed liability for damage caused to already completed work and problems with insurers, but also there is the fact that the Employer is obtaining a principal benefit in advance which may unreasonably delay the eventual issue of the Taking Over Certificate.

However, in road projects, especially rehabilitation projects, it may be unavoidable to prevent use of completed sections of the road before formal Taking Over, particularly if lengthy diversions are not permitted.

Should the Employer take possession before a Taking Over Certificate is issued:

- the part occupied by the Employer is deemed to have been taken over from the date the Employer took possession. Again, this may be in conflict with the local law. In addition, there may be political considerations to be evaluated.

- the Contractor is no longer responsible for the care of the part of the Works taken into the possession of the Employer. The standard Contractors All Risk Insurance policy will almost certainly exclude liability for any damage or loss caused by the Employer's actions. The Contractor should be wary of falling between the requirements of the Contract and the exclusions of the insurers.
- *'If requested by the Contractor, the Engineer shall issue a Taking Over Certificate for this part of the Works.'* No procedure is given and it may be assumed that an appropriate letter of request would be sufficient to require the Engineer to act. Again, this procedure may not be in accordance with local law. It is not in the interest of the Contractor to have the Employer in possession of a part of the site when the assumed handover procedure does not conform to the procedures required by the local law.

The issue of a Taking Over Certificate for a part of the Works results in a reduction of the amount of Delay Damages. The value of the Delay Damages shall be reduced proportionately by the value that the works taken over bears to the Accepted Contract Price. The Engineer may deal with this reduction without further reminder, otherwise the Contractor should request the Engineer to make a determination in accordance with Sub-Clause 3.5 'Determinations'.

10.3   Interference with Tests on Completion

'If the Contractor is prevented for more than 14 days from carrying out the Tests on Completion' (refer to Clause 9) *'by a cause for which the Employer is responsible, then the Employer shall be deemed to have taken over on the date on which the Tests on Completion would have been completed. The Engineer shall then issue a Taking Over Certificate and the Contractor shall complete the Tests on Completion as soon as practical.*

Should the Contractor suffer delay and/or incur cost as a result of this delay in carrying out the Tests on Completion, the Contractor shall give notice to the Engineer in accordance with the requirements of Sub-Clause 20.1, copy to the Employer and be entitled to an extension of time and payment of costs. After receiving this notice, the Engineer shall proceed in accordance with Sub-Clause 3.5 "Determinations".'

10.4   Surface Requiring Reinstatement

As part of site clearance and removal of surplus materials, the Contractor will be required to reinstate surfaces to their original condition or to a condition acceptable to the Employer.

Typically, any work to be carried out under this heading, if not complete at the date of Taking Over, will be included in a list of outstanding works to be attached to the Taking Over Certificate.

Clause 11 Defects Liability

11.1   Completion of Outstanding Work and Remedying Defects

The term 'Defects Liability Period' is defined in Sub-Clause 1.1.3.7 as 'the period for notifying defects in the Works ...'. The period is given in the Appendix to Tender and is calculated from the date of issuance of the Taking Over Certificate (Sub-Clause 10.1 refers).

At the expiry date of the Defects Liability Period, the Works shall be in the condition required by the Contract (fair wear and tear accepted).

During the Defects Liability Period, the Contractor is required to:

(a) *'complete any outstanding work stated in a Taking Over Certificate within a reasonable time as instructed by the Engineer.'* Self-evidently, it is preferable for all the Parties that the outstanding work is completed as quickly as possible and not allowed to drag out over the full Defects Liability Period.

(b) *'Execute all works to remedy all defects or damage as may be notified by the Employer (or Engineer on his behalf) during the Defects Liability Period.'* The defects must be defects relating to the Contractor's obligations under the Contract. Not infrequently disputes arise in respect of responsibility for defects. The cause of a defect should be noted and recorded. The Contractor is not responsible for defects which arise from improper use or inadequate maintenance of the Works by the Employer. Neither is the Contractor responsible for the consequences of fair wear and tear.

The Contractor is not responsible for damage to the Works caused by the Employer or others permitted to use the Works by the Employer including the general public. However, the Contractor remains responsible for any damage caused by his own employees and subcontractors completing any activities during the Defects Liability Period. It is important in this period that the Contractor works in an orderly and controlled manner in order that his employees do not cause further damage while carrying out their tasks.

The satisfactory completion of any outstanding work and the rectification of defects and repairs should be formally recorded and signed-off by the Parties. Periodic joint inspections of the Works by the Parties during the Defects Liability Period would be beneficial, particularly for larger and more complex projects.

11.2   Cost of Remedying Defects

The Contractor is responsible for all costs arising out of his obligations to correct defects and repair damages that are within his contractual responsibility. If the work is attributable to another cause, the Contractor shall be notified promptly by the Employer or Engineer under the Variation procedure of Sub-Clause 13.3. If the Contractor receives such a notice without reference to Sub-Clause 13.3, he is obliged to carry out the work and make claim for payment following the procedures of Sub-Clause 20.1.

Any work notified under this heading must be within the scope of the Works. The Contractor is under no obligation to carry out works outside the scope of Works although there is nothing to prevent the Parties making separate agreements for any extra contractual work.

11.3   Extension of Defects Notification Period

Occasionally it may happen during the Defects Liability Period that the Works, Section or a major item of Plant cannot be used as intended due to a defect or damage. The Employer is entitled to an extension of the Defects Liability Period corresponding to the period of non-serviceability. The extension is limited to the defective item and not to the whole of the Works or Section. The extension period is not to exceed two years.

11.4   Failure to Remedy Defects

'If the Contractor fails to remedy any defect or damage in a reasonable time, a date may be fixed by the Employer by which the defect or damage is to be remedied. The Contractor shall be given reasonable notice of this date. If the Contractor fails to remedy the defect or damage by this notified date and provided the remedial work was to be carried out at the cost of the Contractor, then the Employer may:

(a) carry out the work himself or others at the Contractor's expense.' The Employer is obliged to follow the procedures of Sub-Clause 2.5 'Employer's Claim'.

(b) 'require the Engineer to agree or determine a reasonable reduction in the Contract Price in accordance with Sub-Clause 3.5 "Determinations"'

(c) 'if the defect or damage deprives the Employer of substantially the whole benefit of the Work or any major part of the Works, terminate the Contract as a whole or in part. The Employer shall then be entitled to' recover all sums paid for the Works together with financing costs and costs of dismantling and demobilising the Site. This is self-evidently a very extreme situation and will rarely occur. Legal advice would be essential if such a situation were to arise.

11.5   Removal of Defective Work

If the defect or damage cannot be remedied on Site, the Contractor can remove the effective items for repair with the consent of the Employer. The Employer may require additional security to be provided as a condition of giving consent.

11.6   Further Tests

'Should the remedying of defects and damage affect the performance of the Works, the Engineer has the right to instruct repetition of any of the tests *described in the Contract. These tests shall be carried out at the risk and cost of the Party liable for the cost of the remedial works*' (refer to Sub-Clause 11.2).

11.7   Right of Access

The Contractor has the right of access to the Site for the purpose of rectifying defects and damage. For reasons of security the Employer may impose controls and restraints on the Contractor's activities.

It would be advisable for the Contractor to minimise the possibility of having to work under restrictive security procedures as the inconvenience and disruption can increase the Contractor's costs disproportionately.

11.8   Contractor to Search

The Contractor shall, '*if required by the Engineer, search for the cause of any defect*', or, by extension, the circumstances of any damage. The Engineer is to direct this operation.

Should the Contractor be liable for the defect or damage, then he shall carry out the search at his own cost. If the Contractor is not liable, then he is entitled to be '*reimbursed the cost of the search plus profit to be determined by the Engineer*' (refer to Sub-Clause 3.5 'Determination').

If the cause is disputed, the Contractor is advised to keep detailed records and make a claim under Sub-Clause 20.1.

11.9   Performance Certificate

The obligations of the Contractor under the Contract are not complete '*until the Engineer has issued a Performance Certificate*' (which shall state the date on which the Contractor completed his obligations).

The Performance Certificate shall be issued within 28 days after the latest of the expiry dates of the Defects Notification Periods.

'*Only the Performance Certificate shall be deemed to constitute acceptance of the Works.*' There is no formal action required by the Contractor. However, a close, cooperative relationship with the Engineer would be beneficial, particularly if the Employer is unreasonably influencing the Engineer in the performance of his obligations under this sub-clause.

11.10   Unfulfilled Obligations

Notwithstanding the issue of the Performance Certificate there will remain unfulfilled obligations between the Parties. The most significant of these will relate to the settlement of financial matters and resolution of any remaining disputed issues.

The Employer is to return the Performance Security to the Contractor within 21 days of the date of the Engineer issuing the Performance Certificate.

11.11   Clearance of Site

Most contractors will remove from site their equipment, surplus materials, temporary works etc. as soon as possible. Alternatively, the Contractor may be allowed to use the Site (by agreement with the Employer) as a storage point pending removal of the Contractor's property to another project.

However, upon receiving the Performance Certificate, the Contractor is required to remove his remaining property within a further period of 28 days, unless agreed otherwise with the Employer. Failure to do so entitles the Employer to dispose of and sell the Contractor's property and to restore the Site. The Employer would be entitled to recover his costs and pay only the residual amounts to the Contractor.

Frequently the Contractor may locate some part of his establishment outside the Site on land not belonging to the Employer. The Employer has no jurisdiction in respect of these external areas.

Clause 12 Measurement and Evaluation

This clause is based on the principle that the Works are to be valued by measuring the quantity of each item of work and by applying the appropriate rate given in the Bill of Quantities. Lump-sum contracts with various characteristics are also in use and are discussed in Clause 14. Cost-plus contracts are also a possibility, but are rarely encountered.

12.1   Works to be Measured

The Engineer is to give notice to the Contractor's Representative when he requires any part of the Works to be measured and the Contractor is required to support and attend the Engineer. The Works are to be measured based on these records by the Engineer and agreed by the Contractor.

If the Contractor disagrees with the Engineer's records and/or measurement, he shall give notice of his disagreement to the Engineer. The Engineer shall review the records and confirm or vary them. If the Contractor remains in dispute with the Engineer's records and/or measurement, he is obliged to give a second notice of dispute to the Engineer within a further period of 14 days, otherwise the Engineer's records and/or measurement are considered accurate and correct.

In practice the structured approach described above is rarely adhered to. It is the Contractor who has the vested interest in ensuring that the measurement of work performed is maximised and, equally importantly, that it is measured as quickly as possible after execution for inclusion in the next Interim Payment Application.

Whilst the Engineer may equally have the intention to measure the Works accurately and fairly, he is not under the same economic pressures as the Contractor. As a consequence, it is the Contractor who drives this measurement process and is prepared and able to commit resources to accomplish measurement as soon as practicable.

Significant portions of the measurement may be made from the Drawings, but other operations such as major earthworks, particularly if construction is spread over a long period of time, may require a number of field surveys to be made as a basis for measurement.

Not all items of work are visible or accessible after their execution. In such cases agreed measurement records must be progressively prepared and maintained. Equally, owing to site vagaries, additional operations may have had to be performed that cannot be later discerned from the As-Built Drawings.

Experienced site staff will recognise the crucial need to maintain accurate records of measurement, which should be updated as appropriate.

Wherever possible and whenever items of work are completed, the measurement should be finalised and not left for agreement at some future, undefined date. Memories can be selective and unreliable. In addition, there may be changes in the relevant staff of both Engineer and Contractor, which may further delay finalisation of measurement. The Contractor should be particularly wary, since replacement Engineer's staff may not be receptive to agreeing earlier measurement not formally agreed by their predecessors. It is the Contractor who suffers financially and who is obliged to protect his interests by giving the issue of measurement its due priority.

It would be mutually beneficial for the Engineer and the Contractor to agree a standard format for recording agreed measurements prior to the execution of the Works.

In addition to the measurement of the physical works, there are usually a number of administrative bill items contained in the Contract, which are paid according to certified documentation to be provided by the Contractor. Paper items such as receipts, invoices, records of numbers of vehicles provided for the Engineer and similar items have to be securely stored for future reference, particularly if the Contract is to be audited at a later date by third parties.

12.2   Method of Measurement

It is an unfortunate fact that there does not exist an internationally recognised method of measurement. The method of measurement most frequently encountered is the Civil Engineering Standard Method of Measurement sponsored by the Institution of Civil Engineers, but regrettably even this standard is not yet in widespread use.

The Contract is understandably somewhat vague on the issue of method of measurement and states only that 'measurement shall be made of the net actual quantity of each item' and 'the method of measurement shall be in accordance with the Bill of Quantities or other applicable Schedules'.

It is unreasonable to assume that even a contractor with international experience is familiar with local practices in any specific country. Unless he has staff members with appropriate local knowledge he is, in the preparation of the Tender, going to be dependent on intelligent assessment of the Tender documentation. Given the limited time available for the preparation of the Tender, it will be difficult for a tenderer to make more than a brief check of the correctness of the quantities shown in the Bill of Quantities.

However, a tenderer should undertake a review of the descriptions included in the items in the Bill of Quantities to check that they are comprehensive and conform to the technical specifications. Any omissions or anomalies should be immediately formally queried with the Engineer.

Most unreasonably, it frequently happens that a Bill of Quantities will include a general preliminary statement to the effect that the individual bill item descriptions are not to be taken as a full description of the work included in the item. Sometimes this is interpreted by the Engineer to mean that for any work not specifically identified, but necessary because of work descriptions contained in the Specifications, the cost is deemed to be included in the individual bill item or spread over a group of bill items (refer to Sub-Clause 4.11). Further complications can arise when the Specifications contain misplaced references to the Bill of Quantities or in some cases contradict the descriptions in the Bill of Quantities. A tenderer has little option but to carefully review the wording of the Bill of Quantities and report any anomalies. In the absence of a formal standardised Method of Measurement, this remains an unsatisfactory process which hopefully will receive attention from FIDIC and the various trade organisations in the near future.

For the present the FIDIC Contracts Guide contains the following advisory considerations:

'(a) *If the Bill of Quantities includes principles of measurement which clearly require that an item be measured and if the Bill of Quantities does not contain such an item, then an additional Bill Item will be required.*

(b) *If the Bill of Quantities includes (either by reference or specified) principles of measurement which do not clearly require that a particular item of work be measured and the work was described in the Contract and does not arise from a Variation, then measurement does not require an additional Bill Item.*

(c) *If the Bill of Quantities does not contain principles of measurement for a particular item of work and the work was as described in the Contract and did not arise from a variation, then measurement does not require an additional Bill Item.'*

Items (b) and (c) above emphasise the need for the Contractor's estimating office to make a study to ascertain how and where each item of work will be paid for.

12.3   Evaluation

This sub-clause opens with a basic statement that '*the Engineer shall proceed in accordance with Sub-Clause 3.5 ("Determinations") to agree or determine the Contract Price by evaluating each item of work applying the measurement by the appropriate rate or price specified in the Contract. However, a new rate or price is appropriate for an item of work if:*'

(a)

'(i)   *the measured quantity of the item is changed by more than 10% from the quantity in the Bill of Quantities*

(ii)   *this change in quantity multiplied by the unit rate exceeds 0.01% of the Accepted Contract Amount*

(iii) *this change in quantity directly changes the unit cost by more than 1% and*

(iv) *this item is not specified as a "fixed rate item"* '

The above refers to 'changed' quantities indicating that the change can have either a positive or negative effect. Only significant changes are likely to fulfil the above conditions.

or (b)

'(i)   *the work is instructed under Clause 13 "Variations and Adjustments"*

(ii)   *no rate or price is specified in the Contract for this item and*

(iii) *no specified rate or price is appropriate because the item of work is not of similar character or is not executed under similar conditions as any item in the Contract.'*

'*Each new rate or price shall be derived from any relevant rates or prices in the Contract with reasonable adjustments where applicable. If there are no relevant rates or prices, then the price or rate shall be derived from the reasonable cost of executing the work. The Engineer shall determine interim rates and prices pending a final agreement.*'

12.4   Omissions

'*Whenever work is omitted by means of a Variation the value of which has not been agreed, then if:*

(a)   *the Contractor will incur (or has incurred) cost which would have been deemed to be recovered as part of the Accepted Contract Amount*
(b)   *the omission of the work will result (or has resulted) in this sum not forming part of the Contract Price and*
(c)   *the cost is not deemed to be included in the evaluation of any substituted work, then the Contractor shall give notice of claim to the Engineer*' (in accordance with Sub-Clause 20.1) '*and the Engineer shall proceed to determine the cost to be paid to the Contractor.*'

Should the Employer pay for the full cost of an item, he may be entitled to receive it as his property.

Clause 13 Variations and Adjustments

A large proportion of disputes on a project have their origins in the formation and evaluation of Variations. The Contractor is required to proceed expeditiously with the Works and is not authorised to vary the Works without appropriate instructions from the Engineer. These instructions may constitute a Variation as described in Sub-Clause 13.1 'Right to Vary' (which is discussed below). With increasing probability the Conditions of Contract are amended preventing the Engineer issuing Variations without the authority of the Employer. Employers, particularly public authorities, because of their bureaucratic procedures, are invariably unable to respond as quickly as the situation requires. Further, as a consequence of tight budgetary controls often imposed by loan agencies, the whole process leading to the issue of an authorised Variation can be extraordinarily delayed. Payments on account are rarely authorised under these circumstances to the Contractor's detriment.

Regrettably, there are occasions when Variations are issued without the prior agreement or without negotiation with the Contractor. Since most public authorities require the Contractor to sign an official document to formalise a Variation, the situation can become quite fraught. Should the Contractor not be in agreement with the contents of the Variation, he should decline to sign the document, thereby indicating any disagreement. The disputed element of any Variation should be treated by the Contractor as a claim under the provisions of Sub-Clause 20.1. The Contractor is entitled to payment of the undisputed element of a Variation (or award of an extension of time). Regrettably, it is frequently the case that payment continues to be denied to the Contractor as a consequence of the bureaucratic difficulties noted above. In such case the Contractor should consider adding financing charges to the value of his claim.

The Conditions of Contract recognise the difficulties which can arise in respect of Variations. Sub-Clauses 13.1 'Right to Vary' and 13.3 'Variation Procedure' both contain crucial conditional wording.

Sub-Clause 13.1 states in part: '*Each variation* may *include ...*', which contains the implication that it may contain other items in addition. Sub-Clause 13.3 opens with the wording: '*If the Engineer requests a proposal ...*', implying that the Engineer may not necessarily request a proposal.

It may be assumed that the quoted sub-clauses are in some respects for guidance only and that Sub-Clause 13.3 may represent good practice, but is only activated by the Engineer requesting a proposal from the Contractor.

Variations can be instructed in a number of ways. Instructions that vary the Works are frequently contained in revised drawings or specifications issued with the authority of the Engineer. The need for a formal Variation may not be readily recognised and the work executed without authority. This would then contradict any requirement of the Employer to obtain his prior authority before Variations are authorised.

Uncertainties can readily arise in respect of Variations, which can diminish the trust and confidence between the Parties. Good leadership is required from both Employer and Engineer to ensure that the Contractor receives timely varied instructions and is kept informed how and when any financial issues and requests for extension of time will be dealt with.

It is recommended that the Contractor, on receiving instructions that he considers represent a Variation under the Contract, should immediately write a letter to the Engineer stating that he has in his opinion received instructions representing a Variation under the Contract. Appropriate details should be provided. Confirmatory instructions should be requested with due reference to Sub-Clause 3.3(c) 'Instructions of the Engineer'.

It would be hoped that the Employer and/or Engineer will respond in a responsible manner, otherwise the Contractor may have to consider whether to proceed with the varied work, particularly if considerable costs are to be incurred and/or additional time is required.

If there is no meaningful response to the request for confirmatory instructions within a relatively short period and the Contractor has to continue with the varied work, the Contractor should give notice of claim referencing Sub-Clause 20.1 and within the 28-day time limit for notification. This may prove a protective measure only and if matters can be satisfactorily resolved, then the claim can be withdrawn.

It should be noted that many claim settlements are formalised in a document headed 'Variation Order'. This is an administrative convenience of the Employer and need not be resisted by the Contractor, provided that the contents of the document are acceptable to him.

13.1   Right to Vary

'*Each variation may include:*'

(a) '*changes to the quantities of any item of work included in the Contract.*' The quantities of work included in the Bill of Quantities are estimates only. The final measured quantities of work may be different. Conventionally, changes in quantities that arise as a normal consequence of carrying out the originally planned works are measured within the existing bill items. Changes in quantities that arise as a consequence of a Variation are separately measured within the Variation.

(b) '*changes to quality and other characteristics of any item of work.*' Typically, a change in the strength of concrete may be instructed which requires a change in cement content and aggregate grading. Other elements of costs including placement costs may be unaltered.

(c) '*changes to the levels, positions and/or dimensions of any part of the Works.*' The quantities of work may be varied by these instructions. Some reworking is also a possibility.

(d) '*omission of any work*' (not to be performed by others). Reference is to be made to the valuation procedures described in Sub-Clause 12.4. Work that the Employer requires to be omitted from the Contract and performed by others requires that the Employer and the Contractor make a formal supplementary agreement to that effect. A unilateral act by the Employer would be a breach of contract. The Contractor may have already incurred cost in preparing for the execution of the part of the work to be omitted. As a minimum he would be entitled to payment of the profit/risk included in the Accepted Contract Amount.

(e) *'Any additional work, plant, materials or services necessary for the Permanent Works'*. The Engineer is entitled to instruct any additional or varied works necessary for the Works to fully function and meet its intended purpose even if these works were not specifically identified in the Contract Documents.

(f) *'Changes to the sequence or timing of the execution of the Works'*. It may be assumed that the Engineer will issue instructions under this heading only for the convenience of the Employer. Circumstances for such instructions could include changes in design and the requirements of other contractors. The Contractor will need to carefully review the consequences on his own operations. It is noted that this sub-clause only refers to timing of the execution of the Works, but does not allow the Contractor to alter the timing of completion. Acceleration, if required, is covered by Sub-Clause 13.2.

Variations may be instructed by the Engineer at any time prior to issuing the Taking Over Certificate for the Works. Also prior to issuing the Taking Over Certificate, the Engineer may request the Contractor to submit a proposal for additional or varied work which, if formally accepted, would be a Variation to the Contract.

In both cases the Contractor is obliged to carry out the work covered by the Variation, unless he gives notice to the Engineer that he is unable to readily obtain the Goods or the Plant and Equipment required for the Variation. The Engineer may then cancel, confirm or vary his instructions.

The Contractor is not obligated to carry out work not within the scope of the Contract or variation work instructed after issue of the Taking Over Certificate. Often requests for such extra-contractual work arise close to the conclusion of the Works as the Employer uses surplus funds to complete finishing works previously excluded from the scope of the Contract. The Contractor may find it sufficiently profitable to carry out these works regardless of their contractual status.

Any varied work performed in the Defects Liability Period may require a revised pricing structure since the Contractor's cost base existing prior to the issue of the Taking Over Certificate may no longer be applicable. This aspect requires a careful review by the Contractor without undue delay.

13.2   Value Engineering

'The Contractor may at any time submit to the Engineer a written value engineering proposal at his own cost' but he is under no obligation to do so. The proposal has to meet one or more of four given criteria:

- it must accelerate the works
- it must reduce the cost to the Employer
- it must improve efficiency or value to the Employer
- it must otherwise be of benefit to the Employer

The proposal is to be prepared in the manner given in Sub-Clause 13.3 'Variation Procedure', and if accepted, the Contractor shall be responsible for design (if any).

If the proposed change results in a reduction in the contract value of this part, the Contractor shall receive 50% of this value (excluding adjustments under Sub-Clauses 13.7 and 13.8).

13.3   Variation Procedure

'*If the Engineer requests a proposal prior to instructing a Variation, the Contractor shall respond in writing as soon as possible why he cannot comply by submitting:*'

(a) '*a description of the proposed work*' showing modifications to the programme provided under the provisions of Sub-Clause 8.3 and to the Time for Completion

(b) '*a proposal for the evaluation of the Variation*'

The Engineer is to respond as soon as is practical, but the Contractor shall not delay any work waiting for the Engineer's response. Should the Engineer require the Contractor to suspend any part of his operations, he is required to order a Suspension of Work (refer to Sub-Clause 8.8). Any requirement for recording of costs shall be issued to the Contractor by the Engineer. Measurement in respect of Variations is to be in accordance with Clause 12 'Measurement and Evaluation'.

13.4   Payment in Applicable Currencies

'*If the Contract specifies payment in more than one currency*' and in fixed percentages for the whole contract, then the same criteria generally apply to payment for varied works. However, special circumstances may arise particularly in respect of Provisional Sums (Sub-Clause 13.5 refers) where the majority of the Contractor's expenditure may be incurred in different currency proportions. In these circumstances the Contractor would be entitled to payment in the currencies of expenditure.

13.5   Provisional Sums

Where required, Provisional Sums are included in the Bill of Quantities for parts of the Works that are not required to be priced at the risk of the Contractor.

Provisional Sums shall only be used with the written authority of the Engineer.

The Engineer may instruct:

(a) '*works to be executed by the Contractor and valued in accordance with Clause 13.3 "Variation Procedure"*'

(b) works and services to be supplied by Nominated Subcontractors (refer to Clause 5)

The Contractor shall be paid the actual cost together with the sum for overhead charges and profit stated in the Appendix to Tender.

It may be anticipated that the Contractor will be required to provide invoices/receipts in verification of the amount claimed.

13.6   Daywork

Daywork is intended to be used for *'works of a minor or incidental nature'* that cannot be measured and evaluated by any other means under the Contract.

The work shall be evaluated in accordance with the Daywork Schedule, assuming such a document is provided in the Contract. Unfortunately, very frequently the Tender Documents do not provide such a schedule and if the Contractor has failed to provide his own proposals with the Tender, it can be very difficult and tedious to agree unit rates after the event. Whilst some guidance can be provided in some areas by the German Baugeräteliste or the USA Red Book, these documents can rarely be applied to the evaluation of Dayworks in other locations.

Should there be no Daywork Schedule in the Tender Documents, it is appropriate that the Contractor requests the Engineer to clarify matters. Depending on the precise wording of the Instructions to Tenderers, the alternative would be for the Tenderer to include his own Daywork Schedule in his offer.

The UK adopts a different practice which is based on a standardised Daywork Schedule. Tenderers are required to provide a percentage adjustment (plus/minus) to the rates given in the Standard Daywork Schedule. An estimate of the total value of Dayworks forms part of the Contractor's tender offer for tender-evaluation purposes.

It is the accepted practice that the costs of miscellaneous hand-tools, protective clothing etc. are to be included in the daywork-labour rates. Tenderers should clarify the cost of transporting workers (including idle time) to the place where the daywork will be executed, whether it is to form part of the labour rates or whether the transport and driver will be paid for separately. If there is no separate provision for these costs, then the daywork-labour rates will need to be significantly enhanced to cover these costs.

Frequently site disputes arise concerning the value and applicability of unit rates for labour.

In summary:

- the direct cost of labour includes wages, allowances, leave pay, sick pay, protective clothing, union contribution, pension contributions
- the gross cost of labour is essentially the direct cost plus the Contractor's overhead costs including profit and risk
- the daywork rate for labour is the gross cost as above plus an allowance for travel time, idle time, suspension and any other factor directly related to the performance of dayworks

The Contract requires the Contractor to provide the Engineer with daily records of resources used in the previous day's work. It frequently happens in international construction that the language of the Contract is the English language, but not all low-level supervisors have adequate language skills to keep records of the standard required. The Contractor's Representative is well advised to ensure that standardised report forms are available for use by the supervisors. Plant and Equipment fleet numbers and employee company-badge numbers can be used to assist the supervisor to overcome language difficulties. A standard form is provided for guidance (Appendix F refers).

It will be noted that this standard form can be utilised in a variety of situations where the Contract requires the Contractor to keep records to support his claims, particularly those where the Contractor is entitled to receive payment of cost.

13.7   Adjustments for Changes in Legislation

'*The Contract shall be adjusted to take any increase or decrease in cost resulting from a change in the laws of the country.*'

Tenderers are deemed to have included in their Tender Price the consequences of legislation in force on the Base Date.

In order to comply with the time limitations imposed by Sub-Clause 20.1, it is most important that the Contractor promptly obtains information concerning changes in legislation having an effect on the Contract Price. It should not be overlooked that changes in legislation can occur in the period between the Base Date and award of Contract, when the Contractor may not have a presence in the country. Should the validity of tenders be extended, there is an increasing likelihood of new legislation affecting the Contract Price being promulgated.

Most changes in legislation require a formal authorisation by Parliament or a state authority of similar status. The authorisation typically appears within a state publication and it is recommended that the Contractor makes a subscription to such a publication if available. Other sources of information are the major suppliers (e.g. fuels, cement, timber merchants etc.), the trade unions and, not least, the local newspapers. In the preparation of his tender, the Contractor may have already established rates and prices at the Base Date. Evidence of these rates and prices will be required in order to quantify the consequences of any subsequent changes in legislation.

'*If the Contractor suffers (or will suffer) delay and/or incurs (or will incur) additional cost*' as a result of changes in legislation, the Contractor is required to give notice to the Engineer and act in accordance with the procedures given in Sub-Clause 20.1.

Should the change in legislation result in a reduction in the Contract Price, the Employer is required to present his own formal claim to the Engineer in accordance with Sub-Clause 2.5 'Employer's Claims'. Finally, it is to be noted that there may be a partial overlap between the entitlements due under this sub-clause and the entitlements due under Sub-Clause 13.8 'Adjustment for Changes in Cost'.

13.8   Adjustment for Changes in Cost

This sub-clause provides a methodology to adjust the Contract Price as a consequence of changes in costs. There is a general assumption that costs will increase in time. There is a smaller likelihood that costs will decrease. As a general rule, there is normally no adjustment for changes in cost of contracts whose duration is one year or less, presumably on the grounds that contractors should be able to ascertain escalation costs over short durations with reasonable accuracy.

Theoretically, it is possible to evaluate changes in cost with exactitude by maintaining records of every item of expenditure and comparing those with the cost of the same items at Base Date. Clearly, this is a totally impractical procedure and more efficient methods of calculating changes in cost are necessary.

Consequently, in some contracts the Contractor is entitled to claim reimbursement of the actual increase in costs on a limited number of key items only (cement, steel, fuel, bitumen etc.). In such circumstances the Contractor would have to include in his Tender Offer an allowance for all other items not specified. This method of calculation would be particularly suitable for contracts performed in less-developed countries where the Contractor incurs a significant part of his expenditure in that country and yet reliable statistical indices are not available.

The standard FIDIC General Conditions of Contract take this concept to a higher level by use of formulae.

A number of key elements are again specified and coefficients specified for each element, which are intended to represent the estimated proportional value of each element to the total value. The Contractor should be aware that the value of these coefficients provided in the Tender Documents may not be reliable. He is advised to make his own evaluation of these coefficients in the preparation of his Tender.

For each element the Contractor is requested to specify cost indices to be used to evaluate the change in cost of each element from the Base Data to the date of the period to which each Interim payment Application applies.

The Contractor should take care to select indices whose values are readily available from official sources. Other factors which could affect the choice of indices are the currency of payment and the currency in which the Contractor expects to incur most of his expenditure.

Fluctuations in the relative values of currencies are frequently of concern to contractors. Many contracts specify a fixed exchange rate between local and the selected foreign currency. The real exchange rate may during the course of the Contract become markedly different, often to the Contractor's disadvantage. There is no remedy in the standard General Conditions of Contract for currency fluctuations and the Contractor may find it opportune to take precautionary measures. The advance purchase of foreign currency options is one possible course of action to minimise the effects of any currency fluctuations.

Every effort should be made to avoid the use of general indices, such as cost-of-living index which is unlikely to be representative of the changes in cost of material, labour, plant and equipment used in construction. It may be that the cost-of-living index may give a more satisfactory result, but in periods of high inflation of costs, such as that experienced from 2007 to 2008, the end result may be damaging to the Contractor's interests.

Occasionally it may happen that one element of cost may increase dramatically for reasons that could not have been foreseen at the Base Date. Unless this cost element is included in whole or in part of one of the indices used to calculate the changes in cost, the Contractor is left with a problem, since there is no other clause in the Contract that provides an alternative means of compensation. In equity, it is also correct to state that a dramatic decrease in costs would produce the opposite effect. The only remedy may lie in the laws of the country.

The values of the various indices are prepared by the appropriate Government authorities. It takes time to collect, analyse and publish the indices. Typically, there is a delay of 2–3 months before the updated indices are available. In preparing his monthly evaluation of changes in cost (for inclusion in the Monthly Payment Application), the Contractor should use the latest available value of the index as an interim measure to calculate the changes in cost for the months where data is not yet available. These interim values are to be adjusted once the correct values of the indices become available.

Clause 14 Contract Price and Payment

The Contract Price is the value of the Works performed in accordance with the Contract at any stage of the Contract. To facilitate payment to the Contractor, the Contract Price conventionally is calculated at monthly intervals.

14.1   The Contract Price

(a) The Contract Price shall be evaluated in accordance with Sub-Clause 12.3 and is subject to adjustments in accordance with the Contract.

(b) *'The Contractor is required to pay all taxes, duties and fees required to be paid by him.'* The sub-clause also states that these costs shall not be reimbursed. However, it is usually the case that the VAT is excluded from the Contract Price as it is paid directly by the Employer. Also, it is not unusual for the project to be exempt from customs duties and possibly harbour charges. The Instructions to Tenderers and the Particular Conditions of Contract will clarify requirements for these two major items. Other charges including Royalties (Sub-Clause 7.8), charges associated with Protection of the Environment (Sub-Clause 4.8), Municipal Taxes, connection fees, statutory fees for compliance, testing and checking by Government agencies will probably remain at the Contractor's expense. Again, the Instructions to Tenderers and the Particular Conditions of Contract will need to be carefully reviewed.

(c) It is confirmed that all quantities given in the Bill of Quantities are estimates only and subject to remeasurement in accordance with the requirements of Clause 12 'Measurement and Evaluation'.

(d) *'The Contractor shall submit to the Engineer within 28 days of the Commencement Date a proposed breakdown of each lump sum price'*, if any, contained in the Bill of Quantities. This is to enable the Engineer to calculate the values to be included in any Interim Payment Application. This requirement is confined to lump sums, but it is possible that other similar requirements may be stated in the Particular Conditions of Contract in respect of other bill items.

14.2   Advance Payment

'The Employer shall make an advance payment as an interest free loan for mobilisation when the Contractor submits an advance payment guarantee.' A model of this advance-payment guarantee will be provided as part of the Contract Documents.

The detail of the total amount of the advance payment currencies and repayment details will be given in the Appendix to Tender.

In addition to the advance-payment guarantee the Contractor must also provide a Performance Security (Sub-Clause 4.2). Thereafter, the Contractor must make a formal Application for Interim Payment to the Engineer

Chapter 1

requesting the Advance Payment. The Engineer is then required to certify the amounts following the procedures described in Sub-Clause 14.6.

Although not a complicated document, it may take the Engineer and Contractor some time to agree the format of the Contractor's Interim Payment Application and this should be dealt with as soon as possible.

It is recommended that this advance-payment application be given Index 0 as it does not relate to any particular time period. Subsequent applications can then be numbered 1-2-3 ..., representing the value of work performed in the subsequent months of execution of the Contract.

'*If the advance payment has not been repaid prior to the issue of the Taking Over Certificate, then the whole of the balance shall immediately become due and payable by the Contractor to the Employer.*'

The same repayment criteria apply to Clause 15 'Termination by the Contractor' and Clause 19 'Force Majeure'.

It is to be noted that the advance payment is specifically made for the Contractor's mobilisation costs. It is possible that the Contract Documents may contain provision for the Contractor to provide evidence that he has spent the advance payment specifically for this purpose.

14.3   Application for Interim Payment Certificates

The Contractor is required to submit a Statement to the Engineer after the end of each month, showing in detail the amounts to which the Contractor considers himself to be entitled, together with all supporting documents including the report described in Sub-Clause 4.21 'Progress Reports'. The above extract quite clearly entitles the Contractor to include in his application those amounts to which he, the Contractor, considers himself entitled. The preparation of the corresponding Interim Payment Certificate for presentation by the Engineer to the Employer is the duty and responsibility of the Engineer and does not contractually involve the Contractor. Despite this wording, invariably the Engineer and/or the Employer require the Contractor to modify his application to conform to the certification of the Engineer. In some jurisdictions the Employer requires the Contractor to sign the Engineer's Interim Payment Certificate in order to comply with the Employer's internal accountancy procedures. This comment particularly applies where the Employer is a government agency or parastatal company.

This procedure is not provided for in the Conditions of Contract and Employers generally do not consider it necessary to specify their precise requirements by including modified clauses in the Particular Conditions of Contract. Sub-Clause 14.3 clearly states in part (the Contractor shall show) '*in detail the amount [he] considers himself to be entitled ...*'. Doubt may arise that, by signing, the Contractor accepts the Engineer's figures to represent his full entitlement.

Regrettably, this non-contractual process often can obscure and diminish the very real concerns that the Contractor may have in respect of unpaid items and disputes. Under the circumstances described above, it is recommended that the Contractor prepare a further listing of all claims and other unresolved issues and their valuations not included in the Engineer's Interim

Payment Certificate. This letter is to be sent to the Engineer, copy to the Employer, stating that 'the listing is a summary of all claims and unresolved issues and their valuations as at (date) which are not included in the Engineer's Interim Payment Certificate No. ... for the month of ...'.

This listing should be prepared in sufficient detail to comply with the requirements of Sub-Clause 4.21(f), as this will avoid duplication of effort.

The Contractor's Statement shall include:

(a) the estimated contract value of the Works produced up to the end of the month. This is essentially a measurement of the items included in the Bill of Quantities. Most of the measurement will relate to physical work, but some administrative items are likely to require evaluation.

(b) 'any amounts to be added or deducted for changes in legislation (Sub-Clause 13.7) and changes in cost (Sub-Clause 13.8)'

(c) any amount to be deducted for retention to the limit stated in the Appendix to Tender. A partial Taking Over of the Works would entitle the Contractor to a partial return of retention (refer to Sub-Clause 14.9).

(d) 'any amounts to be added and deducted for the advance payment and repayments'

(e) 'any amounts to be added and deducted for Plant and Materials conforming to the requirements of Sub-Clause 14.5'

(f) 'any other additions or deductions due under the Contract' including claims, variations, dayworks

(g) previous certified amounts shall be deducted

It is strongly recommended that the Contractor does not wait until the last day of the month before commencing the preparation of his Statement. Many items can be measured as the work proceeds: field surveys can be made; administrative payment items such as invoices can be prepared in advance etc.

The Contractor should give consideration to commencement of the measurement by the 25th day of each month. Draft copies of the sections of the measurement could be submitted to the Engineer's staff in a progressive manner for checking, the last few items being quickly evaluated at the month's end.

Particularly in respect of uncomplicated projects, the Engineer's measurement staff should not require the full allowed period of 28 days to agree an interim measurement for the purposes of producing a pre-agreed Statement and Interim Payment Certificate. Both the Engineer's and the Contractor's staff entrusted with this task should have a clear understanding of the significance of the word 'interim' as used in this sub-clause. However, it is an unfortunate fact that in many countries even the interim measurements have to be precise and wholly accurate even though they will be out of date before they are finalised.

14.4   Schedule of Payments

The Contract may provide for the Works to include a schedule of payments specifying the instalments by which the Contract Price will be paid.

The schedule could be based on specified payments becoming due on the achievement of defined milestones. Whilst this procedure is administratively convenient, the scope of work required for the completion of a milestone must be carefully defined. Difficulties can arise when the work, although substantially complete, cannot be fully completed for an extended period, causing delay in payment to the Contractor.

Alternatively, the Contract Price may be divided into a number of task-related lump sums. Invariably the Contractor will be required to provide a further breakdown of these lump sums into a convenient number of sub-elements suitable for evaluation of the progress of the Works. It is the usual practice to evaluate these sub-elements as percentages of the lump sums, rather than give them numerical values. The proposed breakdowns should be prepared and agreed with the Engineer as soon as possible after the Commencement Date, particularly if the Employer also has to give his approval.

14.5   Plant and Materials Intended for the Works

This sub-clause provides for the Interim Payment Certificates to include amounts for Plant and Materials that have been delivered to the Site for incorporation in the Permanent Works.

The sub-clause identifies general conditions that have to be met. It is common practice for payments under this sub-clause to be limited to specific items of Plant and Materials identified in the Appendix to Tender (and possibly in the Particular Conditions of Contract). It is not practical for every minor item to be considered, not least because the administrative costs would probably exceed the potential benefits to the Contractor.

In respect of Plant and Materials to be shipped to the Site from another country, two possibilities exist:

(a)   Payment is permitted once the Plant and Materials are shipped but not yet delivered to Site. A bank guarantee similar to that required for Advance Payment (Sub-Clause 14.2) has to be provided. This guarantee has to be valid until the Plant and Materials are on site and safely stored and protected.

(b)   Payment is permitted once the Plant and Materials are on site and safely stored and protected.

The Contractor will be required to produce documentary evidence of costs and evidence demonstrating that the Plant and Materials are in conformity with the Contract. The latter requirement may require test and/or inspection certification on or off the Site.

More commonly the Contract Conditions will permit payment for materials (e.g. cement, bitumen, reinforcement etc.) purchased locally. In addition, payment may be due for permanent materials manufactured on site by the Contractor. Typically, this would include crushed stone, precast items and similar. Again, evidence of cost and evidence of conformity with the contract specifications are required. The cost of materials manufactured by the Contractor will have to be negotiated with the Engineer.

The standard Conditions of Contract state that 80% of the cost of the Plant and Materials on Site will be advanced, but this figure may be amended in the Appendix to Tender or elsewhere in the Contract Documents.

The amounts paid to the Contractor will be reduced as the Plant and Materials are incorporated in the Works and paid through items included in the Bill of Quantities.

Proof of ownership of Plant and Materials can be problematic, particularly if the subcontractors and sub-suppliers are involved. Sub-Clause 7.7 recognises that there may be problems: '*Each item of Plant and Materials shall, to the extent consistent with the Laws of the Country, become the property of the Employer ...*'. This is potentially a complex issue and the Employer may require additional guarantees from the Contractor in order to protect his interests.

14.6   Issue of Interim Payment Certificates

'*No amount will be certified or paid until the Engineer has received and approved the Performance Security (Sub-Clause 4.2 refers).*'

The Engineer shall issue an Interim Payment Certificate '*within 28 days after receiving the Contractor's Statement and supporting documents*'. The Engineer is not obligated to issue an Interim Payment Certificate if the amount payable is less than the minimum amount stated in the Appendix to Tender. He may decide to certify an amount less than the minimum when the Taking Over is accomplished or when the Performance Certificate is due.

'*The issue of an Interim Payment Certificate does not signify the Engineer's acceptance, approval, consent or satisfaction*'.

14.7   Payment (by the Employer)

(a) The Advance Payment shall be made '*within 42 days of issuing the Letter of Acceptance or within 21 days after receiving the Performance Security (Sub-Clause 4.2) and the Engineer's Interim Payment Certificate*' (Sub-Clause 14.2), whichever is the latest.

(b) '*Amounts certified in each Interim Payment Certificate shall be paid within 56 days of receipt by the Engineer of the Contractor's Statement (Sub-Clause 14.3) and supporting documentation*'. Assuming that the Engineer requires the full 28 days for certification permitted by Sub-Clause 14.6, this leaves the Employer with a further 28 days to make payment. For many Employers, particularly those utilising loan funds for payment, this period is likely to be extended as notified elsewhere in the Contract Documents.

(c) The amount certified in the Final Payment Certificate shall be paid within 56 days of receipt by the Employer of this Payment Certificate.

Payments shall be made in the currencies specified in the Contract.

The Contract may be valued only in local currency. It may be assumed that an international contractor is unlikely to participate in a contract where the currency of payment is not fully convertible into foreign currency.

Chapter 1

The Contract may be valued only in local currency which is fully convertible. The Contractor carries the risk that exchange rates between local and foreign currencies may vary to his disadvantage.

Alternatively, the Contract may be valued in a foreign currency (often a foreign convertible currency provided by the loan agencies) and paid either in the country of execution or in a foreign country selected by the Contractor.

A further possibility is that the Contract may be valued in a local currency, but with the proviso that a fixed percentage, selected by the Contractor in his Tender Offer, will be converted into foreign currency and paid in the foreign country selected by the Contractor. A fixed rate of exchange is provided for in the Contract, usually that rate existing 28 days before the Base Date and notified to the Tenderers by the Engineer or Employer. This conversion rate will apply for the full period of the Contract.

From time to time it may happen that additional work may require a unique division between foreign and local currencies. The purchase of a major item of plant for use by the Employer by means of a Provisional Sum may necessitate expenditure entirely in foreign currency. In this situation the Contractor is entitled to be reimbursed his expenditure in foreign currency.

The selected division between the local and foreign payments has to be carefully assessed. Contractors may be expected to plan their operations so that profit accrues in foreign currency and so that they are not left with a significant amount of non-convertible local currency on conclusion.

14.8   Delayed Payment

Should the Contractor not be paid within the time limits specified in the Contract, he shall be entitled to receive financing charges compounded monthly on the amount unpaid for the period of delay. '*These financing charges shall be calculated at the annual rate of three percentage points above the discount rate of the central bank in the country of the currency of payment.*'

Many Employers rely on project financing from external funding agencies with which to make payments to the Contractor. Occasionally it may happen that the Employer experiences administrative difficulties in the timely provision of those funds and is unable to pay the Contractor as required. Funding agencies are reluctant to allow their funding to be used for payment of financing charges to the Contractor.

This has the consequence that the Employer has to pay the interest charges from his own resources. Often funding cannot be made available until an appropriate budget is secured. This may take time to achieve and a short delay in payment may eventually result in a substantial claim by the Contractor.

Also, it may be anticipated that the Employer will request the Contractor to accept payment of interest in local currency even though that may not be the contracted currency of payment. The Contractor's response will doubtless be determined by his own commercial requirements.

Exceptionally, the Contractor is entitled to interest payments without formal notice or certification since it is an issue to be arranged between the Employer and the Contractor. Nonetheless, the Employer may prefer the involvement of the Engineer for administrative convenience.

14.9 Payment of Retention Money

'*When a Taking Over Certificate is issued by the Engineer for the whole of the Works,*' 40% of the Retention Money shall be certified '*by the Engineer for payment to the Contractor. If a Taking Over Certificate is issued for a Section or part of the Works, then a proportion of the Retention Money shall be certified and paid.*' This proportion shall be calculated by dividing the estimated contract value of the section or part by the estimated final Contract Price.

'*Promptly after the latest of the expiry dates of the Defects Notification Periods the outstanding balance of the Retention Money shall be certified by the Engineer and paid to the Contractor.*' If a Taking Over Certificate was issued for a section or part, then the outstanding balance of the Retention Money for sections or parts will automatically be certified and paid when the latest expiry date of Defects Notification Periods is reached. The Engineer is entitled to withhold certification of the estimated cost of outstanding and defective work (Clause 11).

14.10 Statement at Completion

'*Within 84 days after receiving the Taking Over Certificate for (the whole of) the Works, the Contractor shall submit to the Engineer a Statement at Completion showing*'

(a) '*the value of all works done in accordance with the Contract at the date of the Taking Over Certificate.*' This would include the measured works, the value of varied works performed, the value of accepted claims, as well as any amounts due under Sub-Clauses 13.7 'Changes in Legislation' and 13.8 'Changes in Cost'.

(b) '*any further sums which the Contractor considers to be due*'. This would include an estimate of the value of unresolved claims including ongoing measurement disputes.

(c) '*an estimate of any other amounts which the Contractor considers may become due to him under the Contract*'. This would include the value of ongoing events and claims after the date of issue of the Taking Over Certificate. The value of any outstanding work should also be included. It is not for the Contractor to anticipate any future additional work which might be instructed by the Engineer.

It is recommended that the Contractor evaluates the Statement at Completion as accurately as possible. It represents the maximum revenue that could be due to him and equally indicates to the Employer the likely maximum amount of his financing commitment.

Chapter 1

14.11   Application for Final Payment Certificate

'*Within 56 days of receiving the Performance Certificate the Contractor shall submit a draft final statement with supporting documents to the Engineer showing*'

(a) '*the value of all work done in accordance with the Contract.*' This will include the value of measured works, the value of varied works performed, the value of accepted claims, as well as any amounts due under Sub-Clauses 13.7 'Changes in Legislation' and 13.8 'Changes in Cost'. The Performance Certificate cannot be issued until the Contractor has completed all obligations under the Contract. Consequently, it is necessary to value all works performed and accepted for certification and payment.

(b) '*Any further sums which the Contractor considers to be due to him under the Contract otherwise*'. It may be expected that many of the Contractor's claims and other matters will have been resolved to the satisfaction of the Parties by this date. Consequently, it is probable that only the value of unresolved claims need be entered here. Rarely there may be other outstanding issues existing between the Employer and the Contractor which could be usefully included here.

This application represents the full amount that the Contractor considers due to him at the date of issue of the Performance Certificate.

The Engineer is required to review the draft final statement submitted by the Contractor and obtain the cooperation of the Contractor to reach an agreement on all matters. If this process is successful, the draft final statement shall be modified as agreed and re-submitted by the Contractor. This re-submittal is the 'Final Statement'.

'*If it is not possible to reach a final agreement, then the Engineer shall deliver to the Employer an Interim Payment Certificate for the agreed parts of the draft Final Statement.*'

The remaining dispute(s) must then be resolved by a Decision of the Dispute Adjudication Board (Sub-Clause 20.4) or by amicable settlement (Sub-Clause 20.5) or finally by Arbitration.

14.12   Discharge

In continuation of the procedural requirements given in Sub-Clause 14.11, the Contractor is required to submit a written Discharge that confirms that the total of the Final Statement represents full and final settlement of all moneys due to the Contractor under, or in connection with, the Contract. A sample form of Discharge is provided in the FIDIC Contracts Guide.

The Contract is silent on the matter of interest charges that could occur after the Discharge is provided.

14.13   Issue of Final Payment Certificate

As described in Sub-Clause 14.11, the Engineer and the Contractor are required to make every effort to resolve all outstanding issues which will permit the Contractor to provide to the Engineer a Final Statement together with a written Discharge.

'*Within 28 days after receiving the Final Statement the Engineer shall issue to the Employer the Final Payment Certificate stating the final amount due to the Contractor.*' The Engineer shall give credit for amounts previously paid by the Employer and for the value of any amounts to which the Employer is entitled, and notify the Employer of the balance to be paid to the Contractor.

If the Contractor fails to apply for a Final Payment Certificate, the Engineer, after having given 28 days' written notice, shall issue the Final Payment Certificate without the participation of the Contractor.

14.14   Cessation of Employer's Liability

'*The Employer shall not be liable to the Contractor for any matter or thing in connection with the Contract, excepting to the extent that the Contractor shall have included an amount expressedly for it*

(a)   *in the Final Statement and also*
(b)   *except for matters arising after the issue of the Taking Over Certificate (refer Sub-Clause 14.10) in the Statement at Completion described in Sub-Clause 14.10.*'

This sub-clause does not limit any liability of the Employer in respect of his indemnification obligations or liability arising from fraud, deliberate default or reckless misconduct.

14.15   Currencies of Payment

If the Accepted Contract Amount is expressed in local currency only, the proportion and amounts of the local and foreign currencies shall be stated in the Appendix to Tender.

Other payments shall be made in the currency of expenditure. If no rates of exchange are given in the Contract, they shall be those prevailing at the Base Date and determined by the central bank of the country.

The Contractor should give consideration as to how he might protect himself against excessive currency exchange-rate fluctuations during the execution of the Contract.

Chapter 1

Clause 15 Termination by the Employer

15.1   Notice to Correct

'If the Contractor fails to carry out any obligation under the Contract, the Engineer may by notice require the Contractor to make good the failure and to remedy it within reasonable time.'

On receipt of such notice, the Contractor is well advised to take remedial action without undue delay, since the giving of such notice and the Contractor's failure to respond provide the Employer with a potential opening towards eventual termination of the Contract.

If it is the intention of the Engineer to use this sub-clause for the purposes of termination, the Notice to Correct should refer to this sub-clause, describe the nature of the Contractor's failure and give the Contractor a reasonable time in which to rectify the default.

15.2   Termination by the Employer

This sub-clause itemises the causes that will entitle the Employer to terminate the Contract:

(a)   failure to provide a Performance Security (Sub-Clause 4.2)
(b)   failure to comply with a Notice to Correct (Sub-Clause 15.1)
(c)   abandonment of the Contract or demonstration of intention not to proceed
(d)   failure to proceed with the Works *'without reasonable excuse (Clause 8)'*
(e)   *'failure to comply without reasonable excuse with a notice issued under Sub-Clause 7.5 "Rejection" or Sub-Clause 7.6 "Remedial Works"'*
(f)   *'subcontracting of the whole of the Works or assignment of the Contract without the required agreement'*
(g)   bankruptcy or insolvency
(h)   the giving of bribes or other unlawful inducements

'In any of the above events the Employer may, on giving 14 days notice to the Contractor', expel him from Site. In case of bankruptcy or bribery *'the Employer may by notice terminate immediately.*

The Contractor shall leave the Site having delivered any required Goods, Contractor's Documents etc. to the Engineer.' The Employer may then complete the Works or engage others to do so on his behalf. The Employer shall permit the Contractor to remove his Equipment and Temporary Works from Site at the Contractor's risk and expense. Should the Contractor owe money to the Employer, the Employer may sell items to recover the debt subject to local law.

15.3   Valuation at Date of Termination

'As soon as practical after termination by the Employer, the Engineer shall proceed to agree or determine the value of the Works, Goods' and any other

sums '*due to the Contractor*'. The Engineer must not unduly delay this valuation and he must invite the Contractor in writing to participate in the valuation. If the Contractor fails to respond, the Engineer may proceed unilaterally. The valuation should be copied to both the Employer and the Contractor.

It is quite possible that the Engineer's valuation may be challenged in arbitration proceedings and therefore the valuation should be carried out with exactitude. In particular, the Engineer may find it difficult to evaluate the value of temporary works or partially completed works.

15.4   Payment after Termination

After termination the Employer may:

- present his claims in accordance with Sub-Clause 2.5
- withhold further payments to the Contractor until the costs of completing the Works by others, delay damages and any other Employer costs have been established
- recover the additional costs of completing the Works himself or by the use of a replacement contractor. This may be a lengthy process, since the engagement and costing of a replacement contractor may take considerable time to achieve. This delay can be significant if the selection of a replacement contractor itself is subject to a full tendering process, which would normally be mandatory for public authorities.

Thereafter, the Employer, after recovery of his losses, damages and extra costs, shall pay any balance to the Contractor. It is more probable that the Employer's additional costs will far exceed any credits due to the Contractor and that he will as a consequence make a 'call' on the Contractor's Performance Security. Also, it is possible that the Contractor will not have completely repaid the Advance Payment at the date of termination. This will result in the Employer making a 'call' on the Advance Payment Guarantee.

15.5   Employer's Entitlement to Termination

'*The Employer is entitled to terminate the Contract at any time for the Employer's convenience by giving notice of such termination to the Contractor.*' The notice takes effect 28 days after the Contractor receives the termination notice or when the Employer returns the Performance Security, whichever is the later.

The Employer is not entitled to terminate in order to complete the Works himself or to arrange for others to complete the Works.

After termination the Contractor shall cease works and remove his Equipment from Site as required by Sub-Clause 16.3. He is entitled to payment as specified in Sub-Clause 19.6.

Chapter 1

Clause 16 Suspension and Termination by Contractor

16.1   Contractor's Entitlement to Suspend Works

The Contractor may suspend work or reduce the work rate in three circumstances:

(a) a failure of the Engineer to issue an Interim Payment Certificate within the period of 28 days specified in Sub-Clause 14.6

(b) a failure of the Employer to provide reasonable evidence that financial arrangements have been made or will be made in order to pay the Contractor as stated in Sub-Clause 2.4

(c) a failure of the Employer to make payment of the amount due and within the period given in Sub-Clause 14.7

In all cases the Contractor is required to give 21 days' notice of his intention to suspend work or reduce the work rate.

In cases (a) and (b) above, it can be anticipated that there will be disputes concerning the precise date on which the Contractor was entitled to give notice. Case (c) is an event that can be readily demonstrated and is likely to be most used by the Contractor. The Contractor is entitled to claim an extension of the Time for Completion and to payment of cost and reasonable profit. The Contractor is required to adhere to the procedural requirements given in Clause 20.1. Since the Contractor is entitled to recover his costs, the Contractor must ensure that detailed records of suspension or reduced working are maintained and presented to the Engineer for agreement on a daily basis. Should the Engineer fail to agree these records, the Contractor should submit them formally at regular intervals.

16.2   Termination by Contractor

Terminations by the Contractor are invariably linked with financial disputes, particularly with respect to any failure of the Employer to pay amounts due in respect of Interim Payment Certificates. It is crucial for the Contractor that payments due to him under the Contract are made when due. Any unplanned disruption of cash flow will be of prime concern to him. Contractors working in the international market are likely to be protected in part by export guarantee insurances provided by their home government. Cover under this type of insurance is limited in scope. In particular, the insurance may cover only a fixed number of unpaid monthly Interim Payment Certificates. Most contractors will be unwilling to continue to work once that limit is reached.

Unless the circumstances of the Contract are truly extreme, requiring immediate termination by the Contractor, it is unlikely that notice of termination would be given without prior discussion between the Parties. The Contractor is advised to obtain legal advice before terminating the Contract. A termination subsequently judged to be unjustified could constitute a breach of contract.

'*The Contractor shall be entitled to terminate the Contract if:*'

(a) The Employer fails to provide evidence that satisfactory financing arrangements are in place within a period of 28 days following a request from the Contractor (refer to Sub-Clause 2.4). The Contractor shall then give notice under Sub-Clause 16.1 (Contractor's Entitlement to Suspend Work). The Employer has 42 days to provide the requested evidence, whereafter the Contractor may then give 14 days' notice of termination.

(b) '*The Engineer fails, within 56 days after receiving a Statement and supporting documents, to issue the relevant Payment Certificate.*' The Contractor may then give 14 days' notice of termination (56 + 14 = 70 days after receipt of Statement).

(c) '*The Contractor does not receive the amount due under an Interim Payment Certificate within 42 days*' of the latest date of payment. The Contractor may then give 14 days' notice of termination (42 + 14 = 56 days from latest date of payment).

(d) '*The Employer substantially fails to perform his obligations under the Contract*'. A failure could include failure to provide Site and similar key issues. The Contractor may then give 14 days' notice of termination.

(e) '*The Employer fails to comply with Sub-Clause 1.6 "Contract Agreement" or Sub-Clause 1.7 "Assignment".*' The Contractor is required to give 14 days' notice of termination.

(f) '*A prolonged suspension affects the whole of the Works*' (refer to Sub-Clause 8.11 for periods of notice). The Contractor may give notice of immediate termination (84 + 28 = 112 days from the date of suspension).

(g) '*The Employer becomes bankrupt or insolvent*' or otherwise cannot continue with the Contract. The Contractor may give notice of immediate termination.

The FIDIC Guide advises that if the Contractor gives notice and then wishes to withdraw the notice, the Parties may agree that the notice shall be of no effect and that the Contract is not terminated. If the notice has become effective, then this proviso is presumed to be ineffective. Legal advice should be obtained by the Contractor at all stages of the termination process.

16.3   Cessation of Work and Removal of Contractor's Equipment

The Contract may be terminated by the Employer (Sub-Clause 15.5 refers) or by the Contractor (Sub-Clause 16.2 refers). In addition, the Contract may be terminated under Sub-Clause 19.6 'Optional Termination, Payment and Release'. After a notice of termination has taken effect, '*the Contractor shall promptly:*

(a) *cease all further work*' (except for work for protection of life or property instructed by the Engineer)

(b) *'hand over Contractor's Documents, Plant, Materials and other work for which the Contractor has received payment'*. If payment has not been made, it follows that the Contractor can remove items not paid for from site

(c) *'remove all other goods from Site'*

It is possible that the Employer may seek to prevent the Contractor from removing his Equipment from Site, particularly if he considers that Termination by the Contractor is not justified. If later it is proven that the Employer acted improperly, the Contractor would be entitled to claim reimbursement of all costs arising as a consequence of the improper prevention by the Employer. Again, it is important that legal advice is obtained by both Parties at an early stage.

16.4   Payment on Termination

If the Contract is terminated by the Contractor under the provisions of Sub-Clause 16.2 (Termination by the Contractor), then the Employer shall promptly:

(a) *'return the Performance Security to the Contractor*

(b) *pay the Contractor in accordance with the provisions of Sub-Clause 19.6 (Optional Termination, Payment and Release)*

(c) *pay the Contractor the amount of any loss of profit or other loss or damage sustained by the Contractor as a result of this termination.'*

It is possible that the Contractor's right to terminate will be disputed by the Employer. Resolution of such a dispute may involve the DAB and lead to eventual arbitration. Resolution can be expected to take considerable time to achieve with significant, high costs. It is important that the Engineer promptly measures and values the Works after termination, a process in which the active participation of the Contractor is strongly recommended. In addition, the Contractor should prepare a detailed report on all other matters that may not be subject to the Engineer's measurement and evaluation, and formally submit the same to the Employer and the Engineer as expeditiously as possible.

Clause 17 Risk and Responsibility

The Conditions of Contract variously set out the division of risk and responsibility between the Parties. This clause sets out these risks and responsibilities in some detail. Each Party is required to protect the other Party from claims including those from third parties, arising out of the Contractor's execution of the Works.

The following Clause 18 describes in detail the obligation of the insuring party or parties to cover the risks allocated to them by this Clause 17. Consequently, the risks have to be fully understood and analysed. Detailed engineering studies may be necessary to quantify those risks, particularly for large and complex projects. The services of insurance specialists can be essential for such projects.

17.1   Indemnities

The Contractor is required to indemnify the Employer, the Employer's Personnel and their respective agents against all claims, losses and expenses in respect of:

(a) *'bodily injury, disease or death of any person whatsoever arising out of or by reason of the Contractor's design if any and the execution and completion of the Works, unless attributable to any negligence, wilful act or breach of the Contract by the Employer, his personnel or agents'*

(b) *'damage to or loss of property to the extent that such damage or loss*
   - *arises out of, in the course of the Contractor's design (if any) and the execution and completion of the Works and*
   - *is attributable to any negligence, wilful act or breach of the Contractor, Contractor's Personnel or their respective agents ...'*

The Employer *'shall indemnify the Contractor, the Contractor's Personnel and their agents against and from all claims, damages, losses or expenses in respect of:*

(1) *bodily injury, sickness or death which is attributable to any negligence, wilful act or breach of the Contract by the Employer, the Employer's Personnel or agents and*

(2) *the matters for which liability may be excluded as described in subparagraphs d (i), (ii) and (iii) of Sub-Clause 18.3 "Insurance Against Injury to Persons and Damage to Property"'*

17.2   Contractor's Care of the Works

The Contractor is responsible for *'the care of the Works and Goods from Commencement Date until the Taking Over Certificate is issued, when responsibility passes over to the Employer. If a Taking Over Certificate is issued for a section or part of the Works, responsibility for the care of the section or part passes to the Employer.'*

The Contractor will remain responsible for the care of any work which is outstanding on the date of the Taking Over Certificate until the outstanding work is completed. If loss or damage happens to the Works during the period in which the Contractor is responsible for their care, the Contractor shall rectify the loss or damage at the Contractor's risk and cost.

The Contractor is liable '*for any loss or damage caused by any actions performed by the Contractor after a Taking Over Certificate is issued,*' unless the loss or damage was due to any of the Employer's risks listed in Sub-Clause 17.3. If a Section or part is taken over, it is important that the Section or part is clearly defined.

The Contractor should avoid becoming involved in any maintenance operations of the Employer without a clear agreement of the allocation of risk and responsibility.

17.3   Employer's Risks

Employer's Risks may also be Force Majeure events (Clause 19). Employer's Risks events entitle the Contractor to claim extensions of time and cost.

'*The Employer's Risks are:*

(a) *war, hostilities, invasion, act of foreign enemies*
(b) *rebellion, terrorism, revolution, civil war within the Country*
(c) *riot, commotion and disorder in the Country by persons other than the Contractor's Personnel and other employees*
(d) *munitions of war, explosive materials. ...*
(e) *pressure waves caused by aircraft. ...*
(f) *use or occupation by the Employer of any part of the Permanent Works, unless specified in the Contract*
(g) *design of any part of the Works by the Employer's personnel or others for whom the Employer is responsible*
(h) *forces of nature which were Unforeseeable or against which an experienced contractor could not reasonably have been expected to have taken adequate preventative precautions*' (Note: climatic conditions are specifically excluded from the scope of Sub-Clause 4.12 'Unforeseeable Physical Conditions')

17.4   Consequences of Employer's Risks

In the event of an occurrence of one or more of the Employer's Risks listed in Sub-Clause 17.3 'Employer's Risks', the Contractor shall promptly give notice to the Engineer who shall instruct the Contractor in respect of the extent of rectification required.

This notice shall be given in accordance with the procedures described in Sub-Clause 20.1 and the Contractor shall be entitled to an Extension of Time for Completion and payment of costs arising, including reasonable profit.

The Contractor may be entitled to other compensation under Sub-Clause 19.4 (Consequences of Force Majeure).

The Contractor is advised to keep detailed records of any damage incurred and of the costs of rectification and promptly submit them to the Engineer for agreement.

17.5   Intellectual and Industrial Property Rights

This sub-clause provides protection to each Party in respect of breaches of copyright or of other intellectual or industrial property right.

The Employer shall indemnify the Contractor against any claim which is:

(a) '*an unavoidable result of the Contractor's compliance with the Contract*' or
(b) '*the result of the Works being used for a purpose*' not foreseen by the Contract or used in conjunction with anything not supplied by the Contractor (unless such requirement was made known to the Contractor).

'*The Contractor shall indemnify*' the Employer against claims arising out of the '*manufacture, use, sale or import of any Goods or any design for which the Contractor is responsible*'.

In dealings with suppliers of Goods for inclusion in the Permanent Works, the Contractor should take care to ensure that matters falling under the scope of this clause are fully addressed before placing orders. For example, it may be a requirement of the supplier of the Goods that the Employer obtains a licence for continuing operation. Potential difficulties should be identified and clarified with the Employer. Where appropriate, legal advice should be obtained.

17.6   Limit of Liability

'*Neither Party shall be liable to the other Party for the loss of use of any Works, loss of profit or any direct or consequential loss or damage which may be suffered by the other Party in connection with the Contract other than under Sub-Clause 16.4 and Sub-Clause 17.1.*

The total liability of the Contractor to the Employer shall (excluding some relatively minor items) not exceed the sum stated in the Particular Conditions or if not so stated, the Accepted Contract Amount.'

The responsibilities of the Parties may be affected by the applicable law, which may define the duration of liability.

In some jurisdictions the Contract may contain a requirement for decennial liability insurance.

Insurers will doubtless be well aware of any limit of liability, and the actual wording of the insurance should be reviewed carefully to ensure that adequate insurance cover is provided.

Clause 18 Insurance

18.1   General Requirements for Insurance

This sub-clause specifies the following general requirements for insurances to be provided and maintained either by the Employer or by the Contractor.

The Employer is most likely to provide insurances when the Contract is one of a number of contracts required for the construction of a large project. The Employer may consider that he can obtain such insurances at more favourable rates and that the insurances can be tailored to best meet all of his requirements.

The Employer's intention to provide insurances will normally be so stated in the tender documentation. In the absence of information to the contrary, the Contractor would be entitled to assume that the Employer-provided insurances would be in compliance with this Clause 18. Of immediate concern to a tenderer would be the amount of any excess to be deducted from any insurance payments. If an indicative value of the excess is not given, the tenderer has the option of querying this point with the Engineer or stating his assumed value of the excess in his tender.

In standard FIDIC documents the Party providing the insurances is referred to as the 'insuring Party'. Whenever the Contractor is the insuring Party, each insurance shall be effected with insurers and in terms approved by the Employer. Whenever the Employer is the insuring Party, each insurance shall be effected with insurers and in terms consistent with the details annexed to the Particular Conditions.

The insuring Party is obliged to submit to the other Party evidence that the insurances are in force (premium receipts together with copies of the insurance policies).

Further, the insuring Party has the duty to keep the insurers informed of all the relevant changes or events which arise during the execution of the Works and which may directly relate to the terms and conditions of the insurances.

It is required that the insurances shall be in the joint names of the Parties who shall be jointly entitled to receive payments from the insurers. The method of distribution of payments from the insurers between the Parties has to be agreed between the Parties. It may be appropriate for Parties to open a joint bank account to receive payments from the insurers.

18.2   Insurance for Works and Contractor's Equipment

Unless the Employer undertakes to provide the insurances specified in the Contract, then the Contractor is required to insure the Works, Plant, Materials and Contract Documents for not less than the full cost of reinstatement, including cost of demolition, removal of debris and professional fees and profit. For convenience many Employers specify that these insurances shall be for the Accepted Contract Value plus a fixed percentage, usually 15%. The precise percentage increase will be dependent on a number of factors such as potential increases in cost (inflationary costs), increases in the Accepted Contract Value as a consequence of Variations, together with engineering costs, financial costs etc. which will be incurred by the Employer.

The insurances are required to be in place from the date given in the Appendix to the Tender (usually within a fixed period calculated from the Commencement Date) and shall remain valid until the date of issue of the Performance Certificate.

Although this sub-clause groups together Insurance for Works and Insurance for Contractor's Equipment, it is convenient to consider them separately.

(a)   *Insurance for Works*

Experienced insurers of civil engineering projects will be well aware of the fluctuating risk arising during the course of the project. Generally, the financial risk increases as the construction progresses and as the value of the completed work increases. The risk will fall to a significantly lower level at the date of the Taking Over Certificate and, subject to any ongoing legal requirements (for example, decennial insurance), risk will be extinguished at the date when the Performance Certificate is issued.

In evaluating the insurance premium due, the insurers will take note of the extent of the Employer's Risk listed in Sub-Clause 17.3. Further, the Contract may contain provisions concerning specific risks associated with individual projects. For example, with dam projects, the control of water is crucial to performance of the Contract. The Contractor is likely to be responsible for protecting the Works against river flows to a given level (say, a 1 in 10-year flood risk), with the Employer accepting the risk resulting from more serious floods. The Contractor will be required to demonstrate to both the Engineer (if not already shown in the Contract Documents) and to the insurer how he proposes to deal with the risk allocated to him under the Contract. This can be a complex matter involving programming of the Works, nature of temporary works and other site-related construction matters.

If, as stated in the Contract (and not amended in the Particular Conditions of Contract), the Employer and the Contractor are co-insured, clarification is required to establish which Party is responsible for accepting any loss due to 'deductibles' under the policy.

It is standard practice that the Contractor, if he has the responsibility to arrange and maintain the required insurances, will have the further duty during the execution of the Contract to advise the insurers of any changed circumstances that meaningfully affect the risk accepted by the insurers. Typically, the Contractor will be required to provide a periodic report to the insurers detailing the status of the Works and any changes in risk. Changes that eventually increase the final Contract Price or that extend the Time for Completion (whether or not the subject of a formal award of Extension of Time) may entitle the insurers to payment of additional premiums.

The provisions of this sub-clause entitle each Party to make insurance claims, jointly or severally. It can happen that the Employer and the Contractor are not in accord concerning their individual responsibility for the cause of the event leading to the presentation of an insurance claim. In such circumstances the Employer and the Contractor are required to adopt a mature attitude. Neither Party has the right or the need to damage any claim made to the insurers by the other Party. To do so may expose the offending Party to a claim from the other Party. The allocation of responsibility should be left to the insurer who will doubtlessly appoint loss assessors to make that evaluation on his behalf.

Any claim made under this type of insurance policy should be notified to the insurers as soon as possible after the event. Such notification need only describe briefly the event that may lead to a claim and its severity. It may be a condition of the insurance policy that the insurer has the right to view the damage before repair and restoration work commences, subject always to the safety of the Works. In such case the insurer or loss assessor will need to react quickly to the situation.

Under this heading the Contractor is also required to insure the full cost of Plant, Materials and Contract Documents.

(b)   Insurance for Contractor's Equipment

The Contractor is required to insure his equipment for the full replacement value including the cost of delivery to site (which may be significant if the plant is specifically imported for the project).

The value to be insured is the current value including, where appropriate, any customs duties and other taxes and charges paid on importation. Frequently the Contractor is permitted to import Equipment free of local customs duties and taxes for a specific project. The Equipment is to be re-exported on completion. Should an item of equipment be written-off as a consequence of an accident and not re-exported, the residual value may be the subject of customs duties and taxes. The insurance policy should reflect this possibility.

The Contractor has therefore to consider whether the declared value for insurance purposes shall include any exposure to the payment of customs duties and taxes. The premium to be paid may be a lump sum based on a notional expected Equipment valuation averaged for the period of risk, but is more likely to be subject to periodic re-evaluation according to the value of Equipment actually on site.

Some contractors have their own 'pool' Equipment which is allocated to the various projects as and when required. Consequently, the Contractor may have a continuous global insurance covering all his Equipment in all locations without the need to take out a contract-specific insurance. Such global insurance remains subject to the approval of the Employer (refer to Sub-Clause 18.1).

Alternatively, and particularly for large projects often performed by joint ventures, it is normal operating policy that the Contractor's Equipment is owned by the joint venture (whether purchased from the joint-venture partners or from third parties). The insurance policy will therefore need to be specific to the requirements of the project and in the name of the joint venture.

It is a requirement of the Contract that all Equipment belonging to Subcontractors is insured as if the Equipment were owned by the Contractor. The Subcontractor may have his own insurances, but these may not conform to the requirements of the Contract. In any event, such insurances remain subject to the approval of the Employer. Particular attention is to be paid to the hire of local trucks from local subcontractors for site haulage. The existing insurances are unlikely to conform to the requirements of the Contract, potentially leaving the Contractor at risk.

It may be preferable (and economic) to include the Subcontractor's Equipment within the scope of the Contractor's insurance policy, particularly if the period of engagement is reasonably lengthy. The benefit to the Subcontractor would in principle be reflected in his Subcontract rates and prices. To benefit from this, the Contractor should inform the Subcontractor of his intentions prior to requesting him to provide subcontract prices.

Equipment provided by specialist hire companies may be insured automatically as part of the hire agreement. The Contractor should check for conformity with the requirements of the Contract.

18.3   Insurance Against Injury to Persons and Damage to Property

'*Under this Sub-Clause the Insuring Party shall insure against each Party's liability for any loss, damage, death or bodily injury which may occur to any physical property (excluded things insured under Sub-Clause 18.2) or to any person excepting persons insured under Sub-Clause 18.4 which may arise out of the Contractor's performance of the Contract and before the issue of the Performance Certificate.*

The insured amount shall be for a given limit per occurrence as stated in the Appendix to Tender with no limit to the number of occurrences. If no limit is given, this Sub-Clause does not apply. However, there remains a risk to the Contractor and in such circumstances he should consult with an insurance specialist.'

The insurance shall be provided by the Contractor and be in the joint names of the Parties. The insurance shall cover loss and damage to the Employer's property arising out of the Contractor's performance of the Contract.

Excluded from the insurance unless stated otherwise are:

(a) '*the Employer's right to have the Works executed on or to occupy land required for permanent works*
(b) *damage which is unavoidable as a result of the Contractor's obligations to execute the Works*
(c) *a cause listed in Sub-Clause 17.3 "Employer's Risks", except to the extent that cover is available at commercially reasonable rates*' as noted in the commentary under Sub-Clause 18.1. This aspect should be clarified during the tender stage of the project.

18.4   Insurance for Contractor's Personnel

The Contractor is required to insure all of his employees against claims, damage, losses arising from injury, sickness, disease or death.

This form of insurance may in any event be required by the law of the country. The law may impose additional obligations.

In recognition of the poor level of healthcare and social-service facilities existing in less-wealthy countries, many contractors provide, as an inducement, health insurance in excess of those required by law.

The Employer and Engineer are to be indemnified except to the extent that the claim damage or loss arises from an act of negligence on the part of the Employer or the Engineer.

Subcontractors may be allowed to provide their own insurances, but the Contractor remains responsible for compliance with the Contract. Special care should be taken in respect of Subcontractors and Suppliers who are not continuously engaged on the Site.

Clause 19 Force Majeure

19.1 Definition of Force Majeure

The FIDIC Contracts Guide comments that according to the laws of most countries a Party may be relieved from its obligations in a very narrow range of events. However, in standard FIDIC contract forms, the term 'Force Majeure' is more broadly defined as an exceptional event or circumstance:

(a) *'which is beyond a Party's control and prevented the affected Party from performing any of its obligations*
(b) *which such Party could not reasonably have provided against before entering into the Contract*
(c) *which having arisen, such Party could not reasonably have avoided or overcome*
(d) *which is not substantially attributable to the other Party'*

'Force Majeure may include but is not limited to:

- *war, hostilities etc.*
- *rebellion, terrorism, revolution, civil war etc.*
- *riot, commotion, disorder etc. other than by the Contractor's Personnel and other employees*
- *munitions of war, explosive materials*
- *natural catastrophes such as earthquake, hurricane etc.'*

The relationship of this sub-clause to Sub-Clause 17.3 'Employer's Risk' will be noted.

The following criteria need to be satisfied:

(a) it must be exceptional not merely unusual
(b) it must be beyond the control of the Party who is affected by it. Notice is to be given in accordance with Sub-Clause 19.2
(c) the affected Party could not reasonably have provided against it before the Contract was made
(d) the affected Party could not reasonably have avoided or overcome it
(e) it must not have been substantially attributable to the other Party. If it were attributable to the other Party, then the liability of the other Party would not be limited to the consequences of Force Majeure

19.2 Notice of Force Majeure

'If a Party is or will be prevented from performing any of its obligations under the Contract by Force Majeure, then it shall give 14 days notice after the Party became aware (or should become aware) of the event or circumstance.' The notice shall be given to the Employer, copied to the Engineer.

This sub-clause also states that a Force-Majeure event does not excuse any failure to make payment due under the Contract.

19.3   Duty to Minimize Delay

Each Party has the duty to minimise any delay in performance as a consequence of a Force-Majeure event and shall notify the other Party when the effect of the Force-Majeure event comes to an end.

19.4   Consequences of Force Majeure

'If the Contractor is prevented from performing any of his obligations under the Contract' as a consequence of a Force-Majeure event and has given notice in accordance with Sub-Clause 19.2, he 'shall be entitled to' claim an Extension of Time for any delay and payment of any additional cost incurred. The Contractor shall conform to the procedures given in Sub-Clause 20.1. The Contractor is advised to maintain records, agreed with the Engineer, in respect of a period affected by Force Majeure.

19.5   Force Majeure affecting Subcontractor

The Subcontractor's acts or defaults are regarded as the Contractor's acts or defaults. A Subcontractor's unperformed obligation is a Contractor's unperformed obligation.

Consequently, this Clause 19 applies to the Subcontractor in the same manner as it does to the Contractor. Should the Subcontract contain differing terms from, or more favourable terms than, the Contract, this difference has to be resolved between the Contractor and Subcontractor.

19.6   Optional Termination Payment and Release

If as a consequence of a Force-Majeure event the Works are 'substantially prevented for a continuous period of 84 days or for multiple periods totalling 140 days, then either Party may give to the other Party notice of termination of the Contract.' The notice shall take effect 7 days later.

'On termination the Engineer shall determine the value of the Works done and issue a Payment Certificate which shall include:

(a) the amounts payable for any work carried out for which a price is stated in the Contract
(b) the cost of Plant and Materials ordered and delivered to the Contractor, or of which the Contractor is obliged to take delivery. The Plant and Materials shall become the property of the Employer
(c) other costs incurred by the Contractor in the expectation of completing the Works'
(d) the cost of removing the Contractor's property from Site and the cost of transporting the same to his own country
(e) 'the Cost of repatriating the Contractor's staff and labour employed wholly in connection with the Works at the date of termination'

19.7   Release from Performance under the Law

If any event or circumstance (including Force Majeure) makes it impossible for either or both Parties to fulfil their obligations or by law entitles the Parties to be released from further performance, then notice shall be given by either Party to the other Party. '*The Parties shall be discharged from further performance.*'

'*The sum payable by the Employer to the Contractor shall be the same as that payable under Sub-Clause 19.6.*'

Chapter 1

Clause 20 Claims, Disputes and Arbitration

20.1   Contractor's Claims

This sub-clause contains critical instructions to the Contractor which he is required to strictly follow if he intends to proceed with any claim for additional payment and/or for an Extension of Time. It is vital that key personnel of the Contractor are fully versed in the requirements of this sub-clause and apply them from the outset of the Contract.

Crucially, the Contractor shall give notice of claim to the Engineer '*not later than 28 days after the Contractor became aware, or should have become aware, of the event or circumstances*'.

'Claim' may be taken as an assertion of a right or supposed right contained in the Contract (cross-reference to the listing given in Appendix A). An 'event' can be expressed as a 'happening' or 'occurrence', and 'circumstances' could be expressed as a broad change which generally affects the performance of the works (e.g .a change in Government rules and regulations). In any event FIDIC does not seek to distinguish between 'events' and 'circumstances'.

Occasionally Contractors may be uncertain whether a given event or situation, possibly already under discussion with the Engineer, will develop into a claim, necessitating the Contractor to give formal notice of claim. Given the strict time limitations for giving a notice of claim, it is recommended that if in doubt, the Contractor gives a notice of claim regardless of any ongoing discussions. Claims are easily withdrawn, but cannot be resurrected after the time limit for notification has passed.

In considering whether an event or situation does indeed justify the giving of notice of claim, a Contractor needs to take the basic step of identifying which clause of the Contract entitles the Contractor to make that particular claim. A full listing of those contract clauses that permit the Contractor to claim are given in Pages 90–93 of the FIDIC Contracts Guide and itemised here in Appendix A. When giving notice of claim, the Contractor should take care that it is correctly referenced, thereby establishing the essential framework of the claim.

As described above, the Contractor is required to give notice to the Engineer (copy to the Employer) as soon as practical, but not later than 28 days after becoming aware of the relevant event or circumstance giving rise to the claim. The notice must describe the 'event or circumstance' in sufficient detail for the understanding of the Engineer, but otherwise can be a brief letter of notice only. There is no immediate need to state how much additional time or additional payment is required. The Contractor may not yet have all the required information at this early stage.

The Contractor should be wary of events and circumstances arising from matters not immediately known to him. There may have arisen events or circumstances, in the period between Base Date and Award of Contract, not known to the Contractor. Typically, statutory increases in the cost of labour and materials may have taken place in this interim period. The Contractor must have good local intelligence to deal with this type of situation. A subscription to the relevant government publication can only be beneficial to the Contractor.

The notice is to be sent to the Engineer at the address given in the Contract and by the appropriate means of communication given in Sub-Clause 1.3 (which may exclude the use of e-mail). The original notice should not be sent to the Engineer's Representative on site unless specifically provided for in the Contract, although he should be sent a copy, not least because he will be required to agree site records in many instances.

It is required that the Contractor maintains contemporary records which may be necessary to substantiate both the fact and quantum of the claim. It would be mutually beneficial if the Engineer were to agree with those records, even if liability was not accepted ('Record Purposes Only').

Within 42 days after the Contractor became aware (or should have become aware) of the event or circumstance giving rise to the claim, the Contractor is required to provide the Engineer with a fully detailed claim including all supporting particulars on which the claim is based, together with the Extension of Time and additional payment claimed. It is to be noted that if the Contractor gave notice on the 28th day after the event, he has only a further 14 days to substantiate and evaluate the claim. The sub-clause does provide some relief by adding '... *Or within such period as may be proposed by the Contractor and approved by the Engineer ...*'. Consequently, if the Contractor were not able to quickly obtain all the necessary data with which to prepare his claim, he would be entitled to request additional time for the preparation of his claim. A typical situation might arise where the Contractor requires statistical data for a particular period which has yet to be published. It would be good practice to discuss such matters well before the 42-day period expires and not wait until the 'very last minute' before making such a request. Should the Contractor fail to present his detailed claim within the stated period, then if the failure prevents or prejudices the Engineer from making a full investigation, the Contractor runs the risk that claims for both Extension of Time and additional payment may be diminished or rejected.

'*If the event or circumstance has a continuing effect, the Contractor shall send further interim claims at monthly intervals*', giving the accumulated delay and/or the total amount of additional payment claimed. A final claim shall be sent within 28 days after the end of the effects resulting from the event or circumstance. For some types of claims (refer to Sub-Clause 13.7 'Adjustment for Changes in Legislation' and Sub-Clause 13.8 'Adjustment for Changes in Cost') the effects may be felt until the end of the Defects Liability Period.

On receiving the Contractor's fully detailed claim, the Engineer shall proceed in accordance with Sub-Clause 3.5 'Determinations' to agree or determine the Extension of Time due to the Contractor (refer to Sub-Clause 8.4) and any additional payment to which the Contractor may be entitled. '*Within a period of 42 days after receiving the Contractor's fully detailed claim, the Engineer shall either approve or disapprove the claim stating his reasons.*' He also may request further particulars. The Engineer is obliged to consult with the Parties prior to making any determination.

The Contractor is entitled to payment of any amount reasonably substantiated. Part payments of claim settlements are difficult for some Employers to deal with administratively, considering also that the Particular Conditions of Contract may prevent the Engineer from authorising any additional payment without the permission of the Employer. The Employer himself may also have to consult with other Parties including any financing agencies.

Consequently, it is possible that the Engineer's determination will itself be delayed or that the implementation of any award will be delayed. Payment to the Contractor is not due until included in an Interim Payment Certificate issued by the Engineer. Consequently, there is no relief available to the Contractor in Sub-Clause 14.8 (Delayed Payment). Nonetheless, the Contractor should continue to evaluate and submit interest calculations as other remedies may be available.

Although the Contractor is sanctioned because of a failure to follow the procedural obligations of this Sub-Clause 20.1, there are no immediate consequences in respect of any procedural failings by the Engineer.

If the Contractor is improperly penalised because of a failure of the Engineer to adhere to the requirements of Sub-Clause 20.1, this should be drawn to the attention of the DAB informally or formally, as appropriate. The only other alternative would be for the Contractor to approach the Employer directly, so that the situation can be rectified without delay.

20.2   Appointment of the Dispute Adjudication Board (DAB)

In the past contractors have repeatedly complained at the increasing decline of the independence of the Engineer not being reflected in the Conditions of Contract. Many employers, notably those in Middle-Eastern countries and former Soviet-Bloc countries, take a very active role in the day-to-day management of projects and have their own control systems, which limit the traditional powers and authority of the Engineer and frequently undermine the structure of FIDIC-based contracts. Although the Engineer may provide advice and guidance, the final decision is frequently made by the Employer. Whilst decisions are generally notified to the Contractor through the Engineer, there remain a number of employers who also take on this task themselves, which can give rise to uncertainties in respect of contractual responsibilities and obligations.

The Contract is an agreement between two equal Parties, each with their rights and obligations. Regrettably, this concept is not appreciated or fully understood by many employers who, often for structural reasons, tend to adopt an attitude of 'master and servant' rather than the intended partnership relationship. Unilateral decisions taken by public-sector employers are frequently difficult to overturn without resorting to the full range of dispute-resolution procedures provided in the Contract.

In the preparation of the 1999 series of contract documents, FIDIC evidently took into account the disquiet of the contracting industry about the reduction in the power and authority of the Engineer and about the growing direct participation by Employers in the day-to-day running of projects.

FIDIC has long had the stated objective of providing model forms of contract wherein the risk is allocated between the Parties in a fair and transparent manner.

To counter the decline in the authority of the Engineer, FIDIC in the 1999 series of contract documents has introduced provision for the appointment of a Dispute Adjudication Board. This concept has existed for some years and has been used by the World Bank, who routinely included provision of a Dispute Resolution Board (DRB) in their own standardised modification of the earlier FIDIC 4th Edition 1987.

In the 1999 Conditions of Contract, now under review, the Engineer retains the authority to evaluate or 'determine' the Contractor's claims. However, concerns remain in respect of the reduction of the powers and authority of the Engineer, who may not be able to act impartially because he may have to make judgements concerning the shortcomings of his own staff (and because he is paid by the Employer).

In the earlier FIDIC 4th Edition 1987, The Engineer's arbitral role was extended to require him to make 'Engineer's Decisions' as a prelude to the commencement of full arbitration proceedings. This role no longer exists in the 1999 series of contract documents and has been replaced by the use of the Dispute Adjudication Board (DAB) which has a more expanded role to play in the resolution of disputes.

The FIDIC 1999 Contract forms envisage the appointment of a Dispute Adjudication Board consisting of either one or three suitably qualified members. If a three-member board is required, then each Party shall nominate one member for the approval of the other Party. The two nominees shall agree upon the third member who shall act as chairman of the Dispute Adjudication Board.

In the FIDIC Contracts Guide, FIDIC expresses the opinion that a one-member DAB may be suitable for a project where the average monthly certificate is valued at USD 1.0 million or less. Consideration should also be given to the complexity of the project. A further variation is the possibility of appointing an ad hoc DAB comprising either one or three members who are appointed if and when a particular dispute arises and whose appointment typically expires once a DAB has issued its decision on that dispute.

Clause 20.2 describes the function and operation of the DAB in detail. The choice of form of the DAB (three-member, single-member or ad hoc) is to be stated in the Appendix to Tender. If the requirements are not stated, clarification should be sought from the Engineer in the period for preparation of tenders, not least because the composition of the DAB will significantly affect the costs to be included in the Contractor's tender.

The likely annual cost of a three-member DAB at 2007 prices are (per member):

monthly retainer 12 months x € 2000 =	€ 24 000
20 days at site x € 1000 =	€ 20 000
travel, accommodation, miscellaneous =	€ 6 000
Total annual cost per member =	€ 50 000
Total annual cost 3-member DAB =	**€ 150 000**

This total cost is to be shared equally between the Employer and the Contractor. Therefore, the cost share attributable to the Contractor is of the order of € 75 000 per annum.

The date by which the DAB shall be appointed is to be given in the Appendix to Tender. Again, if a DAB is to be appointed and no date is given in the Appendix to Tender, the matter should be queried with the Engineer in the period for preparation of tenders. It may be expected that the DAB will be functional for at least the full period corresponding to the Time for Completion. The total cost of the DAB to the Contractor can then be estimated for inclusion in the tender offer.

The Contractor is operating in an extremely competitive industry and may be concerned that competitors are prepared to take the risk that a DAB will not in fact be appointed and that consequently they are excluding the cost from their tender offer.

If not publicised by a question to the Engineer for clarification of some aspect of the DAB, a further tactic would be for the Contractor to publicise in his tender that he has considered the intended appointment of the DAB and offer if possible the name of his proposed nominee to the board. Hopefully, the Employer and the Engineer will then assess if other tenderers have correctly completed their tenders.

Occasionally Employers, although providing for a DAB in the Contract, do not activate the implementation of the DAB procedure either for economic reasons or because they are concerned by the potential influence the activities of the DAB may have on their own authority. This can be compounded by a culture of silent compliance by Contractors who are prone to see the non-implementation of the DAB as cost saving, ignoring the possibility or indeed the probability that the same costs and managerial effort will be expended to resolve disputes by more acrimonious and equally costly methods.

This is a somewhat short-sighted policy, since Sub-Clause 20.8 provides for direct referral of a dispute to arbitration if no DAB is in place – all at a much higher cost.

Contractors hold a wide variety of attitudes towards the engagement and functioning of a DAB. Contractors engaging in smaller projects with less experienced managers tend to be wary of the input required and the cost involved in implementing a DAB. More experienced managers on larger, more complex projects are more likely to have positive attitudes.

It is preferable that the Contractor has a clear policy in respect of DABs. It is reported that DABs have almost a 90% success rate in resolving disputes. The successful implementation of a DAB requires cost and effort, but the overwhelming consensus is that DABs have a positive influence in prevention and resolution of disputes and at a significantly lower cost than full arbitration proceedings.

With experience, the Contractor's senior management should be able to compile a listing of potential DAB members who are acceptable. These may be suitably qualified experts, with whom the Contractor has had previous contact, or who have been recommended by other parties known to the Contractor. It may be that experts, not favoured by the Contractor for whatever reasons, are also identified.

At the lower levels of the Contractor's management team it is occasionally perceived that the expert nominated by the Contractor should in some manner be of a favourable disposition to the Contractor. This is not appropriate thinking. The DAB members on appointment will automatically assert their independence from both Parties. The choice of the nomination should be governed essentially by his professional suitability for the task ahead. The nominee should be suitably qualified, with appropriate experience of the type of construction to be executed. It is likely that the Parties are of different nationalities. Consequently, it may be appropriate that the DAB members are of nationalities different from those of the Parties. The DAB members are required to be proficient in the language of the Contract.

The general procedure for operating a DAB after it established is:

- The Parties periodically provide the DAB with documentation which it is considered will keep the DAB members informed of the progress of the various aspects of the Works, which may or may not be the subject of claims by either Party. The Employer usually provides the necessary documentation on behalf of the Parties to the chairman of the Board, who arranges for distribution to the other board members.
- The DAB periodically visit Site by agreement or to suit particular site events. The Employer conventionally acts as the host on behalf of the Parties.
- During site visits by the DAB, the Parties are invited to present informally to the Board any matter either Party considers relevant to the smooth execution and management of the Works. The DAB may request clarifications, but is not required to make any formal comment. If a particularly intractable problem arises, including claim disputes, the Parties may ask the DAB to informally assist them to resolve any disputes. Consequently, it is important that the Contractor fully prepares himself prior to any meeting in respect of any issue he wishes to discuss with the DAB. He must inform the Employer of his intentions. The same criteria apply to any issue the Employer wishes to discuss with the DAB. Advance knowledge of the intentions of the Parties will facilitate the scheduling of the DAB. An effective DAB can be invaluable by informally resolving disputes, provided always that the Parties are flexible and not holding totally irreconcilable positions.
- If the dispute cannot be informally resolved, either Party has the option to make a formal request for a DAB decision using the procedure given in Sub-Clause 20.4.

20.3   Failure to Agree Dispute Adjudication Board

Occasionally it may happen that there are obstructions to the establishment of the DAB:

(a) failure to agree appointment of the sole-member DAB
(b) failure to nominate a member for 3-member DAB
(c) failure to agree appointment of chairman of DAB
(d) failure to agree appointment of replacement within 42 days after a member of DAB is unable or unwilling to continue

The member or replacement member shall be appointed by the entity or official named in the Appendix to Tender after consultations with the Parties. The standard FIDIC model provides that the President of FIDIC shall be the appointing official. The appointment is final and conclusive. The costs of the entity or official are to be shared equally between the Parties.

20.4   Obtaining Dispute Adjudication Board's Decision

No matter can be referred to the DAB unless it is in dispute. A claim will have been notified and detailed under the provisions of Sub-Clause 2.5 'Employer's Claims' or Sub-Clause 20.1 'Contractor's Claims'. The Engineer is then required to proceed under the provisions of Sub-Clause 3.5 'Determinations' with the objective of reaching an agreement. If no agreement is reached, there is then a dispute which can be referred to the DAB.

If these formal requirements are not followed, there is a possibility that the 'defending' Party may assert that the matter is not yet a dispute and cannot therefore be referred to the DAB.

FIDIC lists four criteria to be applied to establish the existence of a dispute:

- *'after rejection of a final determination*
- *when discussions have been discontinued without agreement*
- *when a Party declines to participate in discussions or reach agreement under Sub-Clause 3.5 "Determinations"*
- *when so little progress is being achieved after protracted discussions.'*

To this listing could be added the failure of the Engineer to adhere to the requirements of Sub-Clause 3.5 and within a reasonable time.

Having established that a dispute exists, a Party can then refer the dispute to the DAB for their decision, referencing this sub-clause. However, as noted above, there may be circumstances where a dispute may arise before a determination has been made. The reference should fully describe the circumstances leading to the dispute with all necessary supporting evidence and setting out precisely how the claimant wishes the DAB to intervene. The reference is to be copied to the Employer and Engineer. A claimant Party will naturally present the dispute in a manner favourable to itself. It may be expected that the other Party will respond highlighting the deficiencies of the claimant Party. In presenting the dispute to the DAB, the claimant Party will need to anticipate the likely response of the other Party. The presentation of disputes (and rebuttals) requires a high level of skill and understanding of all aspects of the Contract, possibly including technical issues.

For a three-member DAB, the DAB is deemed to have received the reference on the date it is received by the chairman of the DAB who will routinely issue a notice of the date of receipt of the reference to the Parties.

The DAB is required to follow the Procedural Rules given in an annexe included in the FIDIC Contracts Guide. Rule 8(a) requires the DAB to *'establish the procedure to be applied in deciding a dispute'*.

The Parties are required to promptly make available any additional information or assistance the DAB may require.

The DAB in making their decision are deemed not to act as Arbitrators.

Within 84 days of receiving the reference, the DAB shall give its reasoned decision referencing this sub-clause. If the issues are complex, the DAB may ask for more time to reach their decision. Should the reference contain a number of topics, the DAB will most likely elect to respond to each in separate decisions. Frequently references for a DAB decision will contain a considerable amount of data, typically referring to complex programme analyses or voluminous data supporting a monetary claim. It is frequently unrealistic to expect the DAB to assimilate and evaluate this information within a period of 84 days, which has probably taken the claimant Party a much longer period to prepare.

Even if not leading to a final agreement, the procedures given in Sub-Clause 3.5 'Determinations' may lead to partial agreement on quantum, leaving the DAB to concentrate on matters of principle. To involve the DAB in the detail of quantum can be counter-productive and the DAB, with the agreement of the Parties, may find it necessary to seek the assistance of experts to assist in the matter of evaluation, all at the cost of the Parties.

If either Party is dissatisfied with the decision of the DAB, either Party may give a notice of dissatisfaction. Neither Party is entitled to commence arbitration unless a notice of dissatisfaction has been given.

If no notice of dissatisfaction is given within a period of 28 days after having received the DAB decision, then the decision shall become final and binding upon both Parties.

20.5   Amicable Settlement

Within a period of 56 days after a notice of dissatisfaction is given, the Parties are required to attempt to settle the dispute amicably before commencement of arbitration. However, if no attempt at amicable settlement is made within the period of 56 days, arbitration proceedings may commence.

No procedure is given for amicable settlement. The Parties are left to arrange their own negotiations. Contractors are likely to be more flexible in any negotiations. Employers, particularly public-service Employers, are likely to be more constricted because they will be mindful of their responsibilities in respect of public funds. Amicable settlements, unless professionally conducted, can also have political overtones in many jurisdictions.

If invited to discussions, the Contractor should ensure that it is clear that such discussions are referenced to the amicable-settlement procedure of this sub-clause and are not discussions of a general nature. The Contractor should make a record of the discussions. Any agreement(s) reached must be carefully recorded and agreed in writing by the Parties.

20.6   Arbitration

If a decision of the DAB has not become final and if the dispute has not been resolved by the amicable settlement provisions of Sub-Clause 20.5, *'then the dispute shall be finally settled by international arbitration'*.

Prior to electing to refer a dispute to international arbitration, the referring Party will necessarily have to make an in-depth review of the presentations and rebuttals made by the Parties to the DAB, and of the reasoning for the DAB's decision. The decision of the DAB will be admissible as evidence in the arbitration.

The members of the DAB are appointed because of their previous experience and expertise in the appropriate types of construction. Most probably the members will have attended training courses for arbitrators and mediators and are well versed in dispute resolution.

The referring party has to evaluate whether or not a better result will be obtained from an arbitration panel with members of similar status to that of the members of the DAB. Legal advice is essential. It has been reported that almost 90% of disputes referred to a DAB result in a settlement of disputes.

It may be appropriate to refer only elements of a DAB decision to arbitration. This tactic may be suitable if there is concern that the amount deemed to be due to a Party is considered manifestly incorrect by the other Party.

The regulations relating to arbitral proceedings vary according to which international rules of arbitration are adopted and will doubtless be conducted by experienced lawyers. Self-evidently, arbitration is a costly process and can consume a very considerable amount of work hours by the Contractor's senior staff.

20.7   Failure to Comply with Dispute Adjudication Board's Decision

Unless allowed by law, neither Party can challenge the DAB's decision after it has become final and binding under the Contract. Should a Party fail to comply with this decision, the other Party, without prejudice to any other rights it may have, may refer the failure itself to arbitration under Sub-Clause 20.6.

20.8   Expiry of Dispute Adjudication Board's Appointment

If a dispute arises between the Parties and there is no DAB in place for whatever reason, the dispute may be referred directly to arbitration. This provision covers the situation that may arise because of the intransigence of one Party who obstructs the establishment of a DAB.

Activities and duties of the FIDIC Contractor's Representative discussed in the same order as they appear in the FIDIC Conditions of Contract

Clause 1 General Provisions

Sub-Clause Reference	Action Required
1.3 Communications	Check which forms of communications are author-ised. If e-mail communication is permitted, decide how proof of receipt will be arranged.
	Establish which communications are to be addressed to the Employer, the Engineer and the Engineer's Representative and which require only to be copied. Direct your staff accordingly (cross-refer to Sub-Clause 3.2).
1.4 Law and Language	Secure the services of a local lawyer and translator.
1.5 Priority of Documents	Arrange for the preparation of a consolidated General Conditions of Contract and Particular Conditions of Contract ('cut and paste'). This will assist understanding and minimise the possibility of errors of interpretation.
1.8 Care and Supply of Documents	Ensure that all original (signed) documentation, e.g. the signed contract document, the tender, insurance policies and similar, are securely stored. Access to these documents is to be restricted. Staff to use pho-tocopies for day-to-day activities.
	For repetitive works, particularly road projects, it would be beneficial if the design data, from which the Documents (Drawings) are developed, were pro-vided by the Employer in electronic form (see also Sub-Clause 4.7). Request clarification at tender stage. This will also facilitate the production of as-built drawings.
1.9 Delayed Drawings or Instructions	If not already established in the tender or discussed in post-tender meetings, establish date(s) by which the Employer and/or Engineer will provide drawings for construction purposes. This is linked to the prep-aration of the Programme (reference Sub-Clause 8.3). Allow sufficient lead time for organising resources, particularly materials.
	The Contractor to give notice of claim should the Works become delayed due to a lack of drawings. ➡ CLAIM

A Contractor's Guide to the FIDIC Conditions of Contract, First Edition. Michael D. Robinson.
© 2011 John Wiley & Sons, Ltd. Published 2011 by John Wiley & Sons, Ltd.

Sub-Clause Reference	Action Required
1.10 Employer's Use of Contractor's Documents	The Employer is entitled to make use of the Contractor's intellectual property. Care should be taken to ensure subcontract documents contain the same obligation.
1.11 Contractor's Use of Employer's Documents	The Contractor may use the Employer's Documents for the purpose of performing the Contract. Permission is required if, for example, the Contractor wishes to use these documents for publicity purposes.

Chapter 2

Clause 2 The Employer

Sub-Clause Reference	Action Required
2.1/2.2 Permits, Licenses or Approvals/ Right of Access to Site	Finalise access routes to site if these are not already established at the Base Date or subsequently. Liaise with local authorities, including police, in respect of truck routeing, noise and other environmental issues. Obtain assistance of Employer as necessary (refer also to Sub-Clause 4.15). Should the Contractor suffer delay and/or incur cost as a result of any failure by the Employer to give right of possession of the Site or access thereto within the time allowed, Contractor is entitled to claim additional costs and time. **➡ CLAIM**
2.4 Employer's Financial Arrangement	The Employer's financial arrangements are generally known at the Base Date. Contractor concerns may arise at a later stage of the project should project spending exceed the available funding. If there are major concerns, the appropriate query is to be sent to the Employer. Care is to be taken to ensure that communications are sent to the correct address.

Chapter 2

Clause 3 Engineer's Duties and Authority

Sub-Clause Reference	Action Required
3.2 Delegation by the Engineer	Unless already advised, formally request Engineer to provide a written statement of powers delegated to the Engineer's Representative (cross-refer to Sub-Clause 1.3). The role of the assistants to the Engineer's Representative also requires clarification.
3.3 Instructions of the Engineer	The Engineer may issue instructions in writing or orally. Oral instructions are most likely to be given at the site with the general intention of avoiding delay. The use of field-instruction books to record site instructions is recommended, otherwise all significant oral instructions will have to be confirmed in formal correspondence by either the Engineer or the Contractor.
	Instructions can include variations as described in Sub-Clause 13.1 (often unwittingly). In such circumstances, agreed records should be maintained in order that the variation can be formalised including payment provisions.
3.4 Replacement of the Engineer	The Contractor is entitled to object to the appointment of a replacement Engineer. Should such a rare event arise, the Contractor is required to provide sound reasons for his objection.
3.5 Determinations	In making his determination, the Engineer is required to consult with the Employer and the Contractor. Detailed, accurate records of any consultations shall be prepared. The agreement of both the Employer and Contractor is required to any proposals made by the Engineer. If the dispute continues and if the Engineer issues a determination that the Contractor is unable to accept, the Contractor is required to give notice of objection within a period of 14 days from the date of the determination. Should the Engineer make only an interim determination, the Contractor should give a notice of his reasoned objections in respect of his disagreement with any part of the interim determination.

Chapter 2

Clause 4 The Contractor

Sub-Clause Reference	Action Required
4.1 Contractor's General Obligations	The Contractor's general obligations will include:

The Contractor's general obligations will include:

- design to the extent provided in the Contract
- provision of all things necessary
- executing health and safety programmes
- method statements describing how the Contract will be executed

The compilation and provision of method statements are likely to form an important task requiring the attention of the Contractor throughout the duration of the Contract.

The Contractor may have included some key method statements in his tender which may require clarification or expansion. A listing of the anticipated method statements is to be drawn up and a priority schedule established, compatible with the proposed programme of works (refer to Sub-Clause 8.3).

The establishment of a priority listing will help avoid overstretching the Contractor's technical staff at a crucial stage of the project.

4.2 Performance Security

The Contractor is required to deliver the Performance Security to the Employer, copy to the Engineer, within 28 days of receipt of the Letter of Acceptance.

The security is to be issued by an entity and from within a country approved by the Employer. The form of the security is usually annexed to the Conditions of Contract. The security is to be valid until the Contractor has executed and completed the Works and the Performance Certificate issued, i.e. there is no specific expiry date unless stated in the Contract.

4.3 Contractor's Representative

The Contractor's Representative should be formally introduced in an appropriate manner to the Employer and the Engineer. Unless the Contractor's Representative is named in the Contract, his appointment is subject to the consent of the Engineer.

Chapter 2

Sub-Clause Reference	Action Required
4.4 Subcontractors	Subcontractors named in the tender offer do not need the consent of the Engineer. In such case the Contractor's Representative should confirm his arrangements. All other subcontractors are subject to the consent of the Engineer. For this purpose a fully documented application should be sent to the Engineer in good time. The Engineer is required to respond within a period of 28 days. A rejection results in a further cycle of request and approval. A pre-discussion with the Engineer is advisable.
4.5 Assignment of Benefit of Subcontract	Subcontract documents are required to include a provision for the assignment of the benefits of the Subcontract to the Employer should the subcontractors' obligations extend beyond the expiry date of the Defects Liability Period.
4.7 Setting Out	The Contractor is to obtain setting-out data from the Engineer. Errors in the data entitle the Contractor to recover his costs and entitle him to an extension of time. **➡ CLAIM**
4.8 Safety Procedures	Contractor to engage a specialist safety officer. Provide equipment. Method statement required. This may have cross-reference to the requirements of Sub-Clause 4.22.
4.9 Quality Assurance	All Q.A. procedures/compliance documents to be prepared and submitted to Engineer for consent.
4.10 Site Data	Review again the Site Data made available by the Employer at Base Date. Note that the Employer is obliged to make available any additional Site Data which becomes available after the Base Date. Interpretation of the Site Data remains the responsibility of the Contractor.
4.12 Unforeseeable Physical Conditions	The FIDIC Contracts Guide explains inter alia that 'physical conditions' include natural sub-surface conditions, natural and artificial physical obstructions. Climatic conditions, such as direct effects of rainfall, are excluded.
	Having encountered an unforeseeable physical condition, the Contractor is required to give notice of claim (refer to Sub-Clause 20.1). **➡ CLAIM**

Chapter 2

Sub-Clause Reference	Action Required
4.15 Access Route	If not identified in the Contract Documents, access routes to site should have been subject to a pre-tender research by the Contractor. Some follow-up may be necessary to comply with the requirements of the local authorities (refer also to Sub-Clauses 2.1 and 2.2).
4.16 Transport of Goods	The Contractor is required to give 21 days' notice to the Engineer of delivery dates of Plant and major items of Goods on site.
4.17 Contractor's Equipment	Contractor's Equipment is to be used exclusively on site. Consent for temporary or permanent removal from site has to be obtained from the Engineer.
4.18 Protection of the Environment	The Contractor may be expected to produce method statements to demonstrate compliance with this sub-clause and local requirements.
4.19 Electricity, Water and Gas	The Contractor has the option to provide his own power and water supplies, which may require the consent of the Engineer, particularly if the Employer's and Engineer's offices are to be connected to those supplies. Supplies from the utility companies or from the Employer will require the Contractor to enter into a formal supply contract with the supplier.
4.20 Employer's Equipment and Free- Issue Material	It is most likely that the supply of these items will be described in detail elsewhere in the Contract Documents. This subject should be reviewed and discussed in detail with the Employer and the Engineer. The Contractor should take care to inspect the Employer's Equipment and Free-Issue Materials prior to accepting delivery.
4.21 Progress Report	The format of the Progress Reports needs to be discussed and agreed with the Engineer as soon as practical after the Notice to Commencement. The preparation of the Progress Reports requires a team effort comprising the input of various parts of the Contractor's organisation. A coordinator is to be appointed to edit and produce the final document. All relevant staff are to be made aware that any tardiness may delay the presentation of Interim Payment Certificates (refer to Sub-Clause 14.3).

Chapter 2

Sub-Clause Reference	Action Required
4.22 Security of the Site	Depending on the complexity of the site, the Contractor may expect to provide a method statement as to how he will secure the site, all subject to the consent of the Engineer.
4.24 Fossils	In the event that fossils and other artefacts are found on site, the Engineer is required to give appropriate instructions to the Contractor. The Contractor shall give notice in accordance with Sub-Clause 20.1. **➡ CLAIM**

Chapter 2

Clause 5 Nominated Subcontractors

The Contractor is entitled to reimbursement of all costs associated with nominated Subcontractors, including the cost of the nominated Subcontractors together with any direct costs incurred by the Contractor plus a percentage for the Contractor's overhead and profit. This percentage is required to be stated in the Appendix to Tender. Occasionally it happens that a percentage is not stated. In such case the omission should be formally queried prior to submission of tenders as it may be later deemed that the Contractor should have included this percentage elsewhere in his tender prices.

Sub-Clause Reference	Action Required
5.1 Definition of "nominated Sub contractor"	Nominated Subcontractors may be identified in the Contract or they may be instructed by the Engineer as a Variation (refer to Clause 13). In the preparation of subcontract agreements, appropriate references to the main Contract are crucial to a clear division of risks and responsibilities between the Contractor and Subcontractor. The Contractor is not obliged to assume any greater responsibility than already included in the Contract. The Contractor has to ensure all costs are fully covered.
5.2 Objection to Nomination	It will be difficult to sustain objections to nominated Subcontractors named in the Contract. There may be occasions when the Contractor wishes to object to additional nominated Subcontractors introduced by means of a Variation. The Contractor is required promptly to submit valid reasons for his objection.

Chapter 2

Clause 6 Staff and Labour

Sub-Clause Reference	Action Required
6.1/6.4 Engagement of Staff/ Labour Laws	The guidance of the local labour office should be obtained as required.
6.5 Working Hours	Working hours for the project are frequently fixed in the Contract Documents and usually reflect the work hours of the local working week. For the most part the Engineer's Representative and his assistants will be remunerated according to these standard hours and are reluctant to work additional hours without additional reimbursement. The Employer is likely to take the view that if the Contractor wishes to work additional hours and if the Engineer is in agreement, then the Contractor must reimburse the additional supervision costs which may be substantial.
	Operations such as quarry work, haulage and summer-time asphalt placement invariably involve a considerable amount of overtime or night work. In the circumstances described above, the matter should be raised as a question to the Engineer in the time allowed for preparation of tenders. Depending on the outcome, the Contractor may have to make appropriate allowance in his tender for payment of the Engineer's costs.
6.6 Facilities for Staff and Labour	The provision of facilities for Staff and Labour requires submittal of design and method statements, especially if on-site residential accommodation is to be provided.
6.7 Health and Safety	Depending on the size and complexity of the project, the Contractor may be required to provide site facilities such as a clinic with paramedic and ambulance back-up. The availability and suitability of local hospitals have to be investigated. All costs are to be included in the Contractor's Tender (refer to Sub-Clause 4.8).
6.8 Contractor's Superintendence	An organogram of the Contractor's organisation is to be drawn up and distributed to the Employer, the Engineer and the Contractor's own staff including Subcontractors.

Sub-Clause Reference	Action Required
6.9 Contractor's Personnel	Consideration is to be given to formal induction of Staff and Labour, particularly for large, complex projects.
6.10 Records of Contractor's Personnel and Equipment	Detailed records are to be maintained of all Equipment on site and its current status. Detailed records are also to be maintained of all Staff and Labour engaged continuously on the Works. Subcontractors shall similarly provide their own records for incorporation. This information forms part of the monthly Progress Report (refer to Sub-Clause 4.21). A standard report form should be prepared and agreed with the Engineer.

Chapter 2

Clause 7 Plant, Materials and Workmanship

Sub-Clause Reference	Action Required
7.1 Manner of Execution	Manufacturers of Plant have the obligation to provide evidence of compliance with the requirements of the Contract at all times.
7.2 Samples	The Contractor is required to submit samples and relevant information to the Engineer for consent and at his own expense. Subcontractors also have the obligation to comply with this sub-clause.
7.3 Inspection	The Contractor is to give notice of inspections at key stages of manufacture. Employer may wish to attend at his own expense.
7.4 Testing	The Contractor is responsible for all testing programmes. Method statements are to be submitted. Refer to standard procedures such as ISO 9002. Regular submittal of test results is to be made to the Engineer. Subcontractors are obliged to conform. A summary of tests actually carried out would form part of the Progress Report (Sub-Clause 4.21(e) refers).
	Should the tests be delayed by the Employer or Engineer, then the Contractor is entitled to claim his additional costs and is entitled to an extension of time. ➡ CLAIM
7.7 Ownership of Plant and Materials	Value of permanent Plant and Materials on site is to be established at monthly intervals for inclusion in monthly Interim Payment Application (also refer to Sub-Clause 8.10).
7.8 Royalties	Royalties, rents etc. are to be paid by Contractor. Include costs in tender calculations. Lease agreements for work areas may be necessary.

Chapter 2

Clause 8 Commencement, Delays and Suspension

Sub-Clause Reference	Action Required
8.1 Commencement of Work	Engineer to give 7 days' notice of Commencement Date. The Contractor is required to start work without delay.
8.3 Programme	Contractor to submit a detailed time programme within 28 days of receiving Notice to Commence. The Engineer has 21 days to give consent or to give notice of non-compliance. Since time is limited at the time of commencement, subsidiary programmes may be submitted at a later date.
	In addition to demonstrating compliance with the general requirements of the Contract, the programme should demonstrate activities and their durations, identify critical and sub-critical items with critical path, resources to be employed, production rates etc. In deciding the detail of the programme, consideration should be given as to how the programme could be re-analysed to demonstrate the effect of both excusable and non-excusable delays.
	Finally, in the event that the programme no longer reflects the actuality of the site, the Engineer is entitled to give notice of need to reprogramme and the Contractor shall promptly submit a revised programme, which among other matters is to demonstrate how any delays will be recovered. The resolution of claims relating to Extension-of-Time claims will be crucial and largely dependent on the quality of the programme.
8.4 Extension of Time for Completion	The progress of the Works may be delayed for a variety of reasons described in various clauses of the Contract. These excusable delays give rise to an entitlement to an extension of time for completion. The Contractor is required to give notice of claim within 28 days of the delay event in accordance with Sub-Clause 20.1. Sub-Clause 8.6 refers to delays that are the responsibility of the Contractor.

Chapter 2

Sub-Clause Reference	Action Required
	The events or circumstances entitling the Contractor to extensions of time are identified in various clauses of the Contract. The provisions of this sub-clause entitle the Contractor to extensions of Time for Completion, provided that notice has been given in accordance with Sub-Clause 20.1. Under the provisions of Sub-Clause 20.1, it is mandatory for the Contractor to have given written notice within 28 days of his intention to claim after the Contractor became aware of the event or circumstance giving rise to the claim. **➡ CLAIM**
8.5 Delay Caused by Authorities	It is advisable to make early contact with the authorities and utility companies to obtain an understanding of the rules and procedures of those organisations and how they may affect the Contractor's operations. Key activities requiring input from the authorities and utility companies should, as far as possible, be identified in the work programme (refer to Sub-Clause 8.3). The Engineer should be kept informed of developments by correspondence or in meetings. In order to make a successful claim under this heading, it is necessary to demonstrate the Contractor's adherence to agreed procedures. Notice of claim shall be given within 28 days of the event or circumstance in accordance with the provisions of Sub-Clause 20.1. **➡ CLAIM**
8.7 Delay Damages	This sub-clause permits the Employer to take direct action against the Contractor, should the Contractor fail to complete the Works within the Time for Completion including any adjustments due under Sub-Clause 8.4; it may be presumed that the Employer has consulted with the Engineer before taking action. The Contractor should promptly give notice of dissatisfaction with the action of the Employer, particularly if it is considered that the Engineer has failed to deal appropriately with any valid requests for extensions of time made by the Contractor.

Chapter 2

Sub-Clause Reference	Action Required
8.8/8.9 Suspension of Work/ Consequences of Suspension	The Engineer may at any time instruct the Contractor to suspend work on part or all of the Works. The Contractor shall give notice of claim within 28 days of the notice of suspension if he considers he is not responsible for the cause of delay. In all circumstances it is essential that the Contractor maintains detailed records of all matters affected by the suspension. **➡ CLAIM**
8.10 Payment for Plant and Materials in Event of Suspension	The scope of the claim noted above is extended to Plant and Materials not yet delivered to site if work is suspended for more than 28 days. Suppliers are to be kept informed and are to provide appropriate data for inclusion in the Contractor's own claim. **➡ CLAIM**
8.11 Prolonged Suspension	Should the suspension exceed 84 days, the Contractor is required to ask permission to recommence. If permission is not given within a period of 28 days, the Contractor has the right to terminate.
8.12 Resumption of Work	On resumption of work the status of the Works, including the Contractor's Plant and Materials, is to be jointly recorded by the Engineer and the Contractor.

Chapter 2

Clause 9 Tests on Completion

Sub-Clause Reference	Action Required
9.1 Contractor's Obligations	The Contractor is to give 28 days' notice of intention to carry out each of the Tests on Completion.
9.2 Delayed Tests	If the Tests on Completion are delayed by the Employer, the Contractor shall give notice of claim (cross-refer to Sub-Clause 7.4). ➡ CLAIM

Chapter 2

Clause 10 Employer's Taking Over

Sub-Clause Reference	Action Required
10.1 Taking Over of the Works and Sections	Contractor is required to make application in writing for a Taking Over Certificate up to 14 days in advance of the likely completion date. The Engineer has 28 days to respond by issuing the Taking Over Certificate or rejecting the application advising the Contractor of the reasons for the rejection. In the event of rejection, the whole process starts again. To minimise the likelihood of rejection, it is advisable that informal pre-inspections are made by the Engineer and Contractor at an early date prior to any formal application. These pre-inspections will minimise the possibility of misunderstandings and disputes arising. Great care should be taken to establish that the FIDIC Taking Over procedures are not subordinate to local legal requirements as is the case in some countries.
10.2 Taking Over of Parts of the Works	The standard FIDIC Contract differentiates between the Taking Over of Sections of the Works that are identified in the Contract and are therefore subject to the Taking Over procedures for the whole or Sections of the Works noted above and Parts of the Works that are subject to Taking Over at the 'sole discretion of the Engineer'.
	If there is any doubt concerning 'Sections' and 'Parts', the estimating office should clarify the issue with the Engineer during the tender period.
	It should be noted that the Employer is not entitled to make beneficial use of any part of the Works not taken over, unless there are specific provisions in the Contract.
	Consequently, it is important to discuss the possibility of a partial Taking Over well in advance of the completion of the relevant part of the Works. **➡ CLAIM**

Chapter 2

Sub-Clause Reference	Action Required
10.3 Interference with Tests on Completion	Should the Employer prevent the execution of the Tests on Completion and if the prevention exceeds 14 days, the Employer is deemed to have taken over on the date when the Tests on Completion would otherwise have been completed. The Contractor should write an appropriate letter to the Engineer requesting action by the Engineer. Should the Contractor incur additional costs, he should keep detailed records and make a formal claim to recover these costs. ➡ CLAIM
10.4/11.11 Surfaces Requiring Reinstatement/ Clearance of Site	Once the Works are taken over by the Employer the Contractor still has an obligation to clear up his temporary works (e.g. offices, workshops, fixed plant, roads and yards). It is recommended that an agreement be reached with the Engineer to include these clearance operations as an outstanding work in an attachment to the Taking Over Certificate (or last Taking Over Certificate if the Works are handed over in sections or parts) (refer to Sub-Clause 11.1).

Chapter 2

Clause 11 Defects Liability

Sub-Clause Reference	Action Required
11.1 Completion of Outstanding Work and Remedying Defects	Following the issuance of a Taking Over Certificate, the Contractor is required to complete outstanding work and remedy defects. It is recommended that the Works are periodically inspected jointly with the Engineer and the outstanding works signed-off, and defects recorded and remedied and also signed-off.
11.2 Cost of Remedying Defects	The Contractor is not responsible for the consequences arising from design defects or damages arising from usage by the Employer (or third parties). The Contractor should request additional payment for the execution of non-contractual works (which may be executed to assist the Employer). ➡ CLAIM
11.6/11.8 Further Tests/ Contractor to Search	Should the Contractor incur additional costs in respect of defects or for which he has no contractual responsibility, including any searches instructed by the Engineer, he is entitled to make a formal claim for reimbursement of any costs incurred. ➡ CLAIM
11.9 Performance Certificate	The issuance of the Performance Certificate does not require a formal application from the Contractor. However, the Performance Certificate is only due when all obligations are met. Therefore, the Contractor should continuously liaise with the Engineer, so that those obligations are met within the allotted period.

Chapter 2

Clause 12 Measurement and Evaluation

Sub-Clause Reference	Action Required
12.1 Works to be Measured	The Conditions of Contract allocate primary responsibility for measurement of the Works to the Engineer. However, Contractors would be ill-advised not to make their own calculations based on agreed records. The Contractor is required to agree any final measurements provided by the Engineer, and notice of any disagreement must be given within a period of 14 days. Interim measurements can, by definition, be adjusted in subsequent measurements. Consequently, there is little point in over-elaborating interim measurements, which are subject to later adjustment, and thus delaying the presentation of the Interim Payment Certificate.
12.2 Method of Measurement	Contract documents frequently contain wording (usually in a preamble to the Bill of Quantities) to the effect that any required work not covered by a specific bill item is deemed to be included (spread over) in other bill items (refer to Sub-Clause 4.11). It is to be noted that this sub-clause does not provide for the Contractor to make a claim in respect of any losses incurred.
	To minimise the possibility of such a situation arising, the estimating office should check that payment for the full scope of the Works (as known at the Base Date) is provided for in the Bill of Quantities. Where appropriate, the Engineer should be requested in the Tender Period to clarify any discrepancies.
12.3 Evaluation	During the evaluation process new rates may be required for a variety of reasons (e.g. no existing rates or prices, significant changes in quantities of work, variations etc.). The wording of this sub-clause requires the Engineer to agree or determine new rates. It is recommended that the Contractor provides his own valuation of these new rates at the earliest opportunity.
12.4 Omissions	The Contractor is entitled to compensation for costs reasonably incurred in the expectation of carrying out work subsequently omitted under a Variation. The Contractor should remain alert, as the omission may be hidden in the issue of revised drawings for example. Notice of claim should be provided by the Contractor (refer to Sub-Clause 20.1). ➡ CLAIM

Chapter 2

Clause 13 Variations and Adjustments

Sub-Clause Reference	Action Required
13.1/13.3 Right to Vary/ Variation Procedure	Variations may be initiated by the Engineer by instruction or by a request for the Contractor to submit a proposal. The Contractor is required to respond without delay. In some circumstances variations may be initiated by the Contractor (refer to the example in Sub-Clause 13.2).

Variations may cover changes in quantities, levels/positions/dimensions, omissions, additional work, or changes in sequence. Changes in quantity, in particular, do not necessarily lead to a formal Variation. Sub-Clause 12.3 describes the most likely situation that will lead to a need for a formal Variation.

Should the Variation lead to additional costs and/or affect the Time for Completion, then the Contractor should give appropriate notice to the Engineer (refer to Sub-Clause 20.1). The Engineer has the authority to unilaterally value Variations (although this may be restricted in any Particular Conditions of Contract). The Contractor should give appropriate notice of any dissatisfaction with any Variation whose value and content are disputed by the Contractor.

Occasionally (and particularly in the latter stages of the project when availability of funds is assured) the Employer may require the Contractor to perform additional works that the Contractor considers to be outside the scope of the Works. The scope of the Works is not always easy to define with precision. One commentator has stated his opinion that the Contractor's obligation extends to the performance of all work necessary to ensure the full intended function of the project. The Contractor is entitled to varied payment and an extension of time as appropriate. Should the additional work be profitable, the Contractor may accept to carry out the work without further discussion. It may be that the additional work is instructed so late that the issue of the Taking Over Certificate is likely to be delayed. In such situation the Contractor should insist that the additional work is treated as an outstanding work to be performed in the Defects Notification Period (refer to Sub-Clause 11.1). ➡ CLAIM

Chapter 2

Sub-Clause Reference	Action Required
13.2 Value Engineering	The Contractor is required to submit full details of any proposal of Value Engineering, including design detail, costing etc. There must be a value to the Employer.
13.5 Provisional Sums	Provisional Sums can only be expended in accordance with the Engineer's Instructions. The Contractor's estimating office should check if a percentage oncost is included in the Appendix to Tender. If no percentage is given, the matter should be queried with the Engineer in the pre-tender period. The danger is that the omission may later be manipulated, so that the Contractor does not receive any percentage oncost. If the percentage is inadequate, an additional allowance should be included elsewhere in the tender. The Contractor must keep records of quotations, receipts, invoices etc. to support payment requests. The Contractor may be required to carry out other physical activities in respect of Provisional Sum materials or services. Again, detailed records are to be maintained. Transport of Provisional Sum materials to site and services provided directly to any Provisional Sum supplier (e.g. accommodation, telephones etc.) are also recoverable and do not form part of the percentage oncost.
13.6 Daywork	Estimating office is to ensure that adequate Daywork rates are given in the Tender. If not, it is recommended that the Contractor provides his own rates, particularly if the estimated value of Dayworks does not affect the tender price. Invariably, it is easier to agree these rates at the outset than it is later in the execution of the Contract.

Sub-Clause Reference	Action Required
13.7 Adjustments for Changes in Legislation	In order to claim additional reimbursement in respect of Changes in Legislation, the Contractor needs to obtain official documentation in support of his claim.
	A subscription to the *Government Gazette* (or similar) is recommended. Additionally, formal statements from major companies such as suppliers of fuels, cement, bitumen are also generally acceptable. At the outset of the Contract a check needs to be made if there have been changes in legislation between Base Date and the Date of Commencement. Fuel prices are particularly prone to constant adjustment. The Contractor is required to give notice of claim in accordance with Sub-Clause 20.1. **➡ CLAIM**
13.8 Adjustment for Changes in Cost	If the Adjustment for Changes in Cost is to be based on indices, the estimating office must choose the selected indices very carefully. Logically, it is advisable to nominate indices valid in those countries where the Contractor will incur the majority of his expenditure, otherwise the Contractor may find currency fluctuations will distort his recovery under this heading.

Chapter 2

Clause 14 Contract Price and Payment

Sub-Clause Reference	Action Required
14.1(d) The Contract Price	If the Contract Price consists of a lump sum or lump sums, the Contractor may be required to provide further breakdowns in order to facilitate the monthly measurement and preparation of the Interim Payment Application.
14.2 Advance Payment	It is a pre-condition of payment of the Advance Payment that the Contractor provides for approval:
	▪ the Advance Payment Guarantee ▪ the Performance Guarantee
	Also, the format of the Interim Payment Application has to be agreed with the Engineer and this should be accomplished at the earliest possible date, preferably during pre-tender negotiations. The use of the FIDIC provided Standard Form is recommended. This should ensure that the benefits of the Advance Payment are available at the earliest possible date.
14.3 Application for Interim Payment Certificates	Calculation of the amounts and quantities for inclusion in the Interim Payment Application should commence before the end of each month in order that the application can be made as close as possible to the month's end. Some sections of the Bills of Quantities lend themselves more easily to pre-measurement than others. It may be more convenient to obtain earliest pre-measurement and payment rather than delay matters negotiating minor measurement items which can be dealt with in the next period of measurement.
	Similarly, negotiation of interim payments due under Sub-Clause 14.3(f) (which includes payments in respect of claims) invariably provides difficulties. Many employers find it difficult to authorise the Engineer to certify interim payments in respect of claims. Further, many employers are reluctant to accept Interim Payment Applications that show payment requests under this sub-clause and in some cases refuse to process the payment. This situation often arises because, in addition to the Contractor's Interim Payment Application and the Engineer's Interim Payment Certificate, the Employer's financial department may also require a commercial invoice. Any differences in the amounts shown may result in the payment process being halted.

Sub-Clause Reference	Action Required
	The production of the monthly Progress Report provides opportunity for the Contractor to present details of all unpaid items (presumed not to be included in the Application for Interim Payment). Refer to Sub-Clause 4.21(f).
	An alternative possibility would be to include the listing of unpaid items to the Application for Interim Payment as an attachment. The Engineer would most likely not action the listing, but at least the Contractor's claims would have been officially recorded.
14.5 Plant and Materials Intended for the Works	Plant and Materials intended for incorporation in the Works entitle the Contractor to claim a further temporary advance payment, typically at a rate of 70–80% of the on-site value derived from invoice values and other formal documentation. Transport and similar costs are to be included in the on-site value.
	As these items of Plant and Materials are progressively incorporated in the Works, the total on-site value is reduced accordingly but will be supplemented by the value of new deliveries.
	At the satisfactory completion of the corresponding work item incorporating these Plant and Materials, their value will reduce to zero. Any remaining surplus items revert to the ownership of the Contractor and have to be removed from site. It is possible that the Employer may have a use for some of these surplus materials for his own maintenance purposes and may be willing to negotiate their purchase with the Contractor.
	On many projects the Contractor may produce materials for inclusion in the permanent works. The on-site value of these materials is also due for advance payment. Most notably this would include aggregates produced by the Contractor. A reasonable on-site value would have to be agreed between Engineer and Contractor. The amounts in stockpile would have to be measured at monthly intervals. It will also be necessary for the Contractor to demonstrate that these materials comply with the quality requirements of the Contract.

Chapter 2

Sub-Clause Reference	Action Required
14.8 Delayed Payment	If the Contractor does not receive payment by due date, he is entitled to receive financial charges compounded monthly and calculated from the last day of payment. The financial charges shall be 3% above the discount rate of the central bank in the country of the currency. Evidence of this discount rate has to be obtained. The Contractor's own bankers may be able to provide this information on a regular basis. No formal notice is required, but it is advised that any default under this sub-clause be treated in the same manner as a claim under Sub-Clause 20.1. The amount due is likely to be paid directly by the Employer separately from any amount certified by the Engineer in an Interim Payment Certificate. ➡ CLAIM
14.9 Payment of Retention Money	The issue of a Taking Over Certificate entitles the Contractor to payment of 40% of the total Retention Money for inclusion in the next Interim Payment Certificate. Taking Over of Sections or Parts of the Works requires that a value of theses Sections or Parts be agreed with the Engineer. The Engineer is entitled to withhold the value of any outstanding works.
14.10 Statement at Completion	Within 84 days of receiving the Taking Over Certificate the Contractor is required to submit to the Engineer a Statement at Completion itemising: (a) the value of works done up to the date of the Taking Over Certificate (b) any further sums that the Contractor considers to be due: this essentially includes the value of all claims and any other unresolved items (c) an estimate of any other amounts that the Contractor considers will become due: the value of outstanding works falls under this heading. The Contractor shall include these amounts in an Interim Payment Application and the Engineer shall certify the amounts due to the Contractor as detailed in Sub-Clause 14.3. Much of the required documentation will have been prepared earlier by the Contractor for other purposes.

Chapter 2

Sub-Clause Reference	Action Required
14.11 Application for Final Payment Certificate	Within 56 days of receiving the Performance Certificate, the Contractor shall submit to the Engineer a draft Final Statement with supporting documents showing: ■ the value of all work done (which would include the value of resolved claims) ■ any further sums which the Contractor considers due to him This latter item is effectively the residual value of unresolved claims and other disputed items. The Contractor's draft Final Statement is then to be discussed with the Engineer. If after such discussions disputes still exist, then the Engineer shall deliver to the Employer an Interim Payment Certificate for those parts of the draft Statement not in dispute. The remaining parts in dispute are to be resolved in accordance with Sub-Clause 20.4 or 20.5.
14.12 Discharge	This follows on from the procedure given in Sub-Clause 14.11. The Contractor, when submitting the Final Statement, is to provide a written discharge confirming that the total of the Final Statement represents the full and final settlement of all moneys due to the Contractor in connection with the Contract. FIDIC provides a sample form of discharge.
14.13 Issue of Final Payment Certificate	Within 28 days of receipt of the Final Statement and a written discharge from the Contractor, the Engineer shall issue a Final Payment Certificate. Amounts not included in this Final Payment Certificate represent the amounts that are still the subject of dispute and that are to be dealt with in accordance with the dispute-resolution procedures given in Clause 20.
14.15 Currencies of Payment	Not all payments are due in the proportions or amounts stated in the Appendix to Tender. Other provisions may apply in the circumstances described in this sub-clause.

Chapter 2

Clause 15 Termination by Employer

Sub-Clause Reference	Action Required
15.1 Notice to Correct	Should the Contractor receive a Notice to Correct, the matter should be taken most seriously. Such a notice represents the Engineer's penultimate warning of dissatisfaction with the Contractor's performance. Action should be taken by the Contractor to remedy the situation, as failure to act may result in Termination by the Employer.
15.2 Termination by the Employer	In the event of Termination by the Employer, the Contractor should obtain legal advice. Termination requires 14 days' notice. The Employer is entitled to take possession of Goods, Contractor's Documents etc. and any item that he has paid for. He is not entitled to take possession of Contractor's Equipment and Temporary Plant, which the Contractor should remove from site without delay. Detailed records are to be kept of the actual on-site status and of actions subsequently taken.
15.3/15.4 Valuation at Date of Termination/ Payment after Termination	The Engineer has the duty to value the Works as soon as possible after Termination. The Contractor is advised to cooperate with this task in order to protect his interests. It is possible that the Employer will call (cash) the Advance Payment Guarantee and/ or the Performance Guarantee if insufficient funds are available as a result of the Engineer's valuation. Surplus funds, if any, are to be returned to the Contractor.
15.5 Employer's Entitlement to Termination	The Employer is entitled to terminate the Contract for his own convenience. Payment to the Contractor is to be determined in accordance with Sub-Clause 19.6. The Contractor is advised to cooperate with the Engineer to ensure that detailed on-site records are maintained.

Clause 16 Suspension and Termination by Contractor

Sub-Clause Reference	**Action Required**
16.1 Contractor's Entitlement to Suspend Work	Should the Engineer fail to certify in accordance with Sub-Clause 14.6, the Contractor, having given 21 days' notice, is entitled to suspend the Works or reduce the rate of work.
	The Contractor is entitled to an Extension of Time in respect of any delay, together with payment of costs plus profit. Notification should be given in accordance with the procedures given in Sub-Clause 20.1. Detailed records are to be maintained to support any Contractor's claim. ➡ CLAIM
16.2 Termination by Contractor	This sub-clause lists seven different circumstances that would entitle the Contractor to terminate the Contract. The most common causes of Termination by the Contractor are:
	▪ the failure of the Engineer to issue a Payment Certificate within 56 days of receiving a Statement and documentation from the Contractor ▪ the failure of the Employer to make payment to the Contractor within 42 days of the time allowed for payment (refer to Sub-Clause 14.7)
	The Contractor must give 14 days' notice of Termination.
16.3 Cessation of Work and Removal of Contractor's Equipment	Following Termination, the Contractor shall hand over to the Employer all Contract Documents, Plant and Materials that have been paid for by the Employer. All other items shall be removed from site. Detailed records shall be maintained in support of any Contractor's claim.
16.4 Payment on Termination	Following Termination, the Employer is to return the Performance Security. Payment to the Contractor is governed by Sub-Clause 19.6. The Contractor is entitled to payment of loss of profit and any other damages sustained as a result of this Termination. ➡ CLAIM

Chapter 2

Clause 17 Risk and Responsibility

This clause of the Contract describes in detail risk and responsibility allocated to the Parties under the terms of the Contract.

In summary, the Employer shall indemnify the Contractor in respect of:

- claims and damages in respect of bodily injury attributable to any neglect or wilful act of the Employer
- claims arising from the Employer's right to have the Permanent Works on the land provided by the Employer
- damage that is the unavoidable result of the Contractor's obligation to construct the Works
- Employer's risks (refer to Sub-Clause 17.3)

Should a risk identified as an Employer's Risk result in loss or damage to the Works, Goods or Contractor's Documents, the Contractor shall promptly give notice (refer to Sub-Clause 20.1) of his entitlement to payment of additional cost and/or an Extension of Time for Completion. **➡ CLAIM**

Except for taking action under the provisions of Sub-Clause 17.3, this clause does not require any specific action by the Contractor's Representative, but it is advisable that he has a working understanding of the obligations described in the clause and understands the relationship to the following Clause 18 'Insurance'. It is to be noted that the Contractor is obliged to complete the Works regardless of the wording of any insurance policy, unless the event giving rise to damage or loss is an event for which the Employer has assumed the risk.

Chapter 2

Clause 18 Insurance

In order to protect himself against the risks allocated to him in Clause 17, the Contractor will be normally required to provide insurances to protect both Parties from the financial consequences of unexpected loss. Occasionally the Employer will elect to provide the required insurances, particularly for larger projects involving a number of individual contracts and contractors.

The negotiation and provision of insurances for civil engineering projects are specialist activities, particularly because each project has its own specific requirements.

Sub-Clause Reference	Action Required
18.1 General Requirements For Insurances	Although generally the insurances are to be taken out by the Contractor, the policies shall be in the joint names of the Parties who shall be jointly entitled to receive payments from the insurers.
	Occasionally the Employer undertakes to provide the contract insurances in whole or in part. Should the Employer fail in his obligations, the Contractor may provide his own insurances and claim reimbursement from the Employer. ➡ CLAIM
	It may be a requirement that the Parties open a joint bank account to receive payments from which distributions shall be made to the individual Party.
	The Parties are required to provide to each other evidence of payment of premiums made to the Insurer.
	Self-evidently, these insurances should be in place before work commences. In complex conditions the insurer may be willing to provide a temporary cover note, valid until preparation of the final insurance document.
	Neither Party should damage the interests and rights of the other Party in respect of any claim notified to the insurers. It may happen that the interests of the Employer and the Contractor differ. Each Party should proceed with caution and avoid attributing blame until such time as the insurers have formally responded to the insurance claim. The Contractor is obliged to promptly notify the insurer of an event that may give rise to a claim under the insurance policy. It is for the insurers to decide if a claim is valid under the terms of the insurance policy.

Chapter 2

Sub-Clause Reference	Action Required
	The insurers may wish to inspect any damage that is the subject of claim and be made aware of any restoration or replacement. The insurer (or his loss assessor) is to be requested to attend site without delay.
	Subcontractors who perform part of the Works will be included in the Contractor's insurances. The Subcontractors should be informed of the nature and detail of the insurance policy in case they wish to take out supplementary insurance policies of their own.
18.2 Insurance for Works and Contractor's Equipment	Insurance for Works and Contractor's Equipment is to be for a sum representing the full reinstatement, repair or replacement cost. The Conditions of Contract may contain a requirement for insured sums to include an additional percentage for the Employer's own costs. Consequential losses are excluded.
	The premiums for insurance of the Works will be based initially on the Accepted Contract Amount and may require adjustment if the Contract Price varies significantly. For his own administrative convenience the Employer may include a contingency allowance and value added tax as part of the Accepted Contract Amount.
	The value of the Contractor's Equipment will also vary as the Works proceed. Depending on the terms of the insurance policy, the Contractor may be required to periodically produce listings and values of on-site Equipment. Premiums may vary according to the actual value of the Contractor's Equipment in use on site.
18.3 Insurance Against Injury to Persons and Damage to Property	The insurable amount is given in the Appendix to Tender. Estimating office should check requirements.
18.4 Insurance for Contractor's Personnel	Insurances for Contractor's Personnel may be supplementary to the health and social provisions of the country in which the Works are to be performed. The Contractor should check carefully the extent of his obligations.
	Expatriate personnel are usually separately insured by the Contractor as part of their individual employment contracts.

Chapter 2

Clause 19 Force Majeure

Sub-Clause Reference	Action Required
19.1/19.2 Definition of Force Majeure/ Notice of Force Majeure	Sub-Clause 19.1 lists five exceptional events or circumstances constituting Force Majeure. The events or circumstances must be exceptional. The criteria of adverse physical conditions which were 'Unforeseeable' as specified in Sub-Clause 4.12 are irrelevant to the definition of Force Majeure.
	In the event of a Force Majeure condition arising, the Contractor's Representative is required to give notice within 14 days of becoming aware (or should have been aware) of the event or circumstance constituting Force Majeure. It is to be noted that this notice period is less than the general notice period given for other claims in Sub-Clause 20.1. ➡ CLAIM
19.3 Duty to Minimise Delay	The Contractor has a general duty to minimise any delay. However, if additional costs will be incurred as a consequence, confirmatory instructions should be obtained from the Engineer in support of any request for reimbursement of those costs.
19.4 Consequences of Force Majeure	The Contractor is entitled to an Extension of Time – refer to Sub-Clause 8.4. Additionally, the Contractor is entitled to payment of costs incurred as a consequence of Force Majeure with two exceptions: ■ costs will not be reimbursed in respect of war hostilities in other countries ■ costs will not be reimbursed in respect of earthquakes, hurricanes or similar 'Acts of God' ➡ CLAIM
19.5 Force Majeure Affecting Sub-Contractor	Subcontractors are also subject to the provisions of this Clause.
19.6 Optional Termination, Payment and Release	Should the event or circumstance be exceptionally severe and execution of the Works is prevented for more than 84 days, either Party may give a notice of Termination. ➡ CLAIM
19.7 Release from Performance Under the Law	Should execution of the Contract become impossible or unlawful, then the Contractor should immediately seek legal advice. Either party will be entitled to release from further performance of the Contract.

Chapter 2

Clause 20 Claims, Disputes and Arbitration

Sub-Clause Reference	Action Required
20.1 Contractor's Claims	The Contractor's Representative requires a clear understanding of this key sub-clause. It is possibly the most important sub-clause relating to contractual issues. Failure to understand or adhere to the requirements of this sub-clause can only damage the interests of the Contractor.

- Notice of claims should be sent to the Engineer no later than 28 days after the relevant event or circumstance, otherwise the Contractor will lose any entitlement.
- Describe the event or circumstance giving rise to the claim. More details can be provided later and separately.
- Ensure that the notice of claim is sent to the correct person at the correct address. Note that the Clause prohibits the Engineer from delegating his authority in making any determination.
- Include reference to claim notices in the monthly report (refer to Sub-Clause 4.21(f)).

There is no specific requirement for the Engineer to respond. Detailed particulars are not required for this initial stage. It is recommended that a claim-numbering system is introduced. Each claim should be given a concise descriptive title, which shall be constantly used thereafter in the heading of any correspondence or other submittals.

Accurate and timely collection of operational records and other relevant data are crucial to the accurate evaluation of many claims, particularly those claims where the Contractor is entitled to reimbursement of cost. Wherever possible, the Engineer should be involved in this process and asked to sign his agreement for 'record purpose only'. Should the Engineer decline to cooperate, then the records will have to be submitted unilaterally.

Sub-Clause Reference	Action Required
	Within 42 days after the Contractor became aware of the event or circumstance giving rise to claim, the Contractor is required to submit detailed particulars which will include a detailed statement and quantum, accompanied by all appropriate documentation. This will require a considerable effort by the Contractor and its preparation should commence as quickly as possible. This is an interim submittal and further submittals are required at monthly intervals, which is unavoidable if the event or circumstance is continuing.
	Within 42 days of receiving a claim (or further particulars if requested), the Engineer shall respond on the principles of the claim. Reasonably substantiated amounts should be included in the next Interim Payment Certificate. Some Employers find it administratively difficult to deal with the concept of an interim payment. The Employer's failure to make payment, when due, entitles the Contractor to add compound interest to the value of the sum due (refer to Sub-Clause 14.8). ➡ CLAIM (procedural)
20.2 Appointment of the Dispute Adjudication Board	The composition of the DAB is given in the Contract Documents. Even as early as the period for tender preparation, it would be appropriate if the Contractor gave thought to the choice of nominee to the DAB. Regrettably, many employers and contractors give low priority to the appointment of the DAB members, which runs counter to the intention that the DAB shall be functional at the commencement of construction.
20.4 Obtaining Dispute Adjudication Board Decision	The Engineer is required to give his determination in accordance with the procedures described in Sub-Clause 3.5, which procedures include consultation with the Parties. If the Engineer's determination is rejected by either Party, then a dispute exists and can be referred to the DAB.

Note

The preparation of submittals to the DAB and later to an Arbitration Board (if necessary) is a specialised activity. This is unlikely to be undertaken by the Contractor's Representative without significant support from specialist staff including lawyers and engineers.

Chapter 2

Activities and duties of the FIDIC Contractor's Representative summarised and arranged in time sequence

A The Estimating Office and Management

Clause No.	Action
General	Prepare report (including video) of the site visit.
1.8	Check if the design data on which the Documents (Drawings) are based is available in electronic form.
2.1/2.2/4.15	Site visit – check access routes to site and any restrictions.
4.2	Make preliminary contact with proposed provider of Performance Security.
4.3	Following award, obtain consent to appointment of the Contractor's Representative if not named in the Tender.
4.4	Consider how many (if any) subcontractors can be named in the Tender submission.
4.10	Obtain copies of the Employer's Site Data.
4.19	Review source of power and water supplies.
5.1	Check if percentage charge for nominated Subcontractors is included in the Appendix to Tender. If not, send clarification query to Engineer.
6.5	Check if the project working hours are fixed by the Contract. Check compatibility with the Programme. Query with the Engineer if necessary and ask for overtime unit rates for the Engineer's staff if overtime is both permitted and unavoidable. Make appropriate allowance in the Tender.
7.8	Check if royalties or rents have to be paid by the Contractor. Make appropriate allowance in the Tender.
10.1/10.2	Check arrangements for Taking Over. Differentiate between Section Taking Over and Taking Over of Parts of the Works.

Chapter 3

A Contractor's Guide to the FIDIC Conditions of Contract, First Edition. Michael D. Robinson.
© 2011 John Wiley & Sons, Ltd. Published 2011 by John Wiley & Sons, Ltd.

Clause No.	Action
12.1/12.2	Review the scope of the Bill of Quantities to ensure that all work items are properly covered. This is particularly important should any Preamble to the Bill of Quantities contain wording to the effect that the cost of any work activity for which there is no specific bill item is deemed to be included in (i.e. spread over) all other bill items. Query with the Engineer as appropriate or make appropriate allowance in the Tender.
13.6	If not provided for in the Tender Documents, consider whether it is appropriate for the Contractor to include his own Daywork rates with his offer. These rates logically have to be higher than the unit rates used to build up the Tender unit prices.
13.8	(a) Maintain a written record of the cost of materials and labour existing at Base Date and used as a basis of Tender, complete with copies of offers, quotations etc. (b) Review carefully the choice of indices. Allow for non-reimbursed escalation.
14.2	Make preliminary arrangements for the provision of the Advance Payment Guarantee in order that it can be obtained at short notice after award of Contract.
18.1	Make preliminary contact with proposed provider of insurances.
20.2	Make first consideration of potential nominee to the DAB. Include cost of DAB in Tender offer.

Note 1
Prepare brief explanatory report of Tender development for the information of the Contractor's Representative.

Note 2
Prepare brief but accurate record of developments and agreements of post-Tender negotiations, particularly those that relate to site activities.

Chapter 3

B Initial Stages of the Project

Note:

A disproportionate number of Contractor's claims arise in the initial stages of a project. Regardless of whether the Employer or the Contractor is ultimately responsible for the cause of delay, the orderly and timely performance of the initial stages of the project are frequently disrupted and made more costly. These delays are not only damaging to the economic performance of the Works, but are often difficult to recover.

Consequently, it is important that, following receipt of the Commencement Date, every effort is made to adhere to the requirements of the Contract as summarised below.

Clause No.	Action
1.3	Check which forms of communications are permitted. Special consideration of e-mail communications may be required. Establish which communications shall be addressed to which Party (cross-refer to Sub-Clause 3.2).
	Establish which communications shall be addressed to which Party (cross-refer to Sub-Clause 3.2).
	Direct your staff accordingly. Establish limitations on direct communication by Contractor's staff with the Engineer and his staff.
1.4	Engage services of a translator and reserve the services of a local lawyer.
1.5	Arrange for preparation of a consolidated General Conditions of Contract and Particular Conditions of Contract ('cut and paste').
1.8	Ensure that all original (signed) documentation, e.g. the signed contract, the tender, insurance policies and similar, is securely stored. Access to be restricted. Staff to use photocopies for day-to-day activities.
1.9	If not established in the Tender or discussed in post-Tender meetings, establish date(s) by which the Employer and/or Engineer will provide drawings for construction purposes. This is linked to the preparation of the Programme (cross-refer to Sub-Clause 8.3).
2.1/2.2/4.15	Finalise access routes to site. Liaise with local authorities, including police, in respect of truck routeing, noise and other environmental issues.
3.2	Request Engineer to provide a written statement of powers delegated to the Engineer's Representative.

Chapter 3

Clause No.	Action
3.3 (and General)	Consider the use of field-instruction books to record site instructions and agreements.
4.1/4.18	Draw up a listing of method statements that are likely to be required. Establish priorities compatible with the Programme.
4.2/14.2	Provide the Performance Certificate and Advance Payment Guarantee to the Employer.
4.4	Obtain consent for Subcontractors not named in the Contract Documents.
4.7	Obtain setting-out data from Engineer.
4.8	Engage special Safety Officer if required. Provide Equipment and Materials.
4.9	List of all Q/A procedures to be prepared and sent to Engineer. (Basic documents may have been included in the Tender submission.)
4.10	Review Site Data. Query whether more Site Data has become available with the Employer since Base Date.
4.19	Organise power and water supplies.
4.21	Agree format of Progress Report with Engineer. Organise system for preparation of Progress Reports.
4.22	Review safety and security of site including facilities. Engineer may require a method statement.
6.1/6.4	The guidance of the local labour office should be obtained as required.
6.5	Review working hours (cross-refer to comment made in Section A for estimating office).
6.6	Arrange accommodation and facilities for Staff and Labour as required.
6.7	Review provisions for medical facilities.
6.8	Prepare and distribute organogram of site organisation.
6.10	Arrange for the preparation and maintenance of records of staff and labour engaged on the Works (see also Sub-Clause 4.21).

Chapter 3

Clause No.	Action
8.1	Commence work without delay after receipt of notice of Commencement Date.
8.3	Prepare and submit detailed Programme of Works.
8.5	Contact statutory authorities to obtain information concerning regulations and procedures that apply to relocated services and other matters.
13.7	Make arrangements for supply of information concerning Changes in Legislation. Subscription to *Government Gazette* if available is recommended. Check whether there have been any changes between Base Date and Commencement Date. Give Notice of Claim if there have been changes (refer to Clause 20.1).
13.8	Make arrangements for supply of value of the indices to be used for evaluation of Adjustment for Changes in Cost.
14.2	(a) Provide Advance Payment Guarantee to Employer. (b) Agree format of Interim Payment Application and submit first application for payment of the Advance.
18.1	Submit evidence of insurances to the Employer.
20.2	In cooperation with the Employer establish a functioning Dispute Adjudication Board. Nominees to be confirmed and formal employment contracts agreed and signed.

Chapter 3

C The Early Stages of the Project and Continuously Thereafter

Clause No.	Action
1.11	Obtain permission of Employer to use photographs and other documents for non-contractual purposes.
2.4	Periodically review the Contract Price to check whether Employer funding is sufficient.
3.3	Discuss with Engineer the use of field-instruction books.
3.5	Prepare for and hold discussions with Engineer as pre-condition to the Engineer making a determination.
4.16	Give 21 days' notice to the Engineer of delivery dates of Plant and major items of Goods to site.
4.20	Hold discussions with Employer and Engineer for the management and inclusion in the Works of Employer's Equipment and Free-Issue Materials (if any).
4.21	Prepare and submit monthly Progress Reports.
6.9	Arrange induction of Staff and Labour with particular reference to health and safety issues.
7.2	Provide samples of Materials and relevant information to Engineer.
7.3	Ensure that Engineer has knowledge of and access to quarries, borrow pits, concrete plant, asphalt plant yards etc. Give notice of any required staged manufacture inspections as Engineer may wish to attend.
8.3	Reprogramme the remaining Works when instructed by the Engineer.
12.1	Delegate staff to work in cooperation with Engineer's staff to measure the works for inclusion in the monthly Interim Payment Application.
12.3	Prepare and negotiate new or adjusted unit rates.
13.1/13.3	(i) Respond to variation proposals initiated by the Engineer.
	(ii) Contractor to provide detailed proposals for any Variation initiated by him.

Chapter 3

Clause No.	Action
13.2	Contractor to provide full details of any proposal of Value Engineering.
13.5	Contractor to action instructions of Engineer concerning expenditure relating to Provisional Sums. A detailed pricing proposal may be required, particularly if the total price is a mixture of lump sums, unit rates, dayworks etc.
14.2/14.3	Prepare Interim Payment Applications and submit to Engineer.
14.5	Prepare monthly valuation of Plant and Materials intended for the Works. Agree unit value rates for any site-manufactured materials (aggregates, precast items etc.). Include value in the Interim Payment Applications.

Chapter 3

D The Latter Stages of the Contract

Clause No.	Action
4.17	Obtain permission for removal of Contractor's Equipment from Site.
9.1/10.3	Give 28 days' notice to Engineer of intention to carry out each of Tests on Completion. It is preferable that a detailed schedule be agreed with the Engineer.
10.1	Make written application for the issue of a Taking Over Certificate. Consider the usefulness of pre-inspections with the Engineer.
10.2	Establish whether the Contract provides only for the issue of a single Taking Over Certificate or whether sectional or partial Taking Over Certificates are specified or permitted.
10.4/11.1/ 11.11	Following the issue of the (final) Taking Over Certificate, clear away all temporary works and restore surfaces as required. Arrange for periodic inspections of the Works taken over in cooperation with the Engineer. Maintain agreed records of outstanding works completed and defects repaired.
11.9	The Performance Certificate can only be issued once all obligations are met. Contractor to ensure that there is no cause for delay in returning this document for cancellation.
14.10	Within 84 days of receiving the Taking Over Certificate, submit a Statement at Completion to the Engineer.
14.11	Within 56 days of receiving the Performance Certificate, submit a draft Final Statement to the Engineer.
14.12	When submitting the Final Statement, the Contractor is required to provide a written discharge.

Chapter 3

E The Ultimate Situation

The Contractor's Representative should be aware that the matters raised under this sub-heading are of such critical nature that not only is the outcome of the individual project jeopardised, but possibly the economic future of the Contractor.

The advice and assistance of a suitably qualified lawyer should be obtained without delay. For all events falling under this sub-heading, the Contractor's Representative is required to ensure that his staff maintain accurate and detailed records of all matters that may develop as a consequence of these critical issues.

Clause No.	Action
15.1	On receipt of a Notice to Correct, the Contractor's Representative should treat the notice most seriously and immediately take all possible action to correct the complaints of the Engineer.
15.2	In the event of Termination by the Employer, he is entitled to take possession of Goods, Contractor's Documents and other items for which he has made payment under the Contract. A formal handing-over document should be drawn up for agreement. The Contractor's Representative should arrange for the immediate removal of the Contractor's Equipment and temporary Plant from site. Detailed records of all removals shall be maintained.
15.3/15.4	Following Termination, the Engineer has the duty to value the Works without delay. The Contractor's Representative is to organise his staff to cooperate with the Engineer. Do not allow the Engineer to take unilateral measurements.
15.5	If the Contract is terminated for the convenience of the Employer, the Contractor's Representative shall follow the same procedures noted above.
16.3	If the Contract is terminated by the Contractor, the Contractor's Representative shall follow the same procedures noted above.
16.4	In the event of Termination by the Contractor, the Contractor's Representative shall ensure that the Employer returns the Performance Security.
18.2	The Contractor's Representative shall arrange for the likely final Contract Price and the value of the Contractor's Equipment to be revalued at regular intervals. The insurer may require this information as there may be a revision of the insurance premium.

Chapter 3

Clause No.	Action
19.7	Should the execution of the Contract become impossible or unlawful, the Contractor may, after receiving appropriate legal advice, give notice of release from further performance.

F Claims

In order for the Contractor to make a claim under the terms of the Contract, it is necessary to identify a clause of the Contract that entitles the Contractor to make that claim. A full listing of the clauses of the Contract entitling the Contractor to make a claim is given in Appendix A. For completeness, a listing of the clauses entitling the Employer to make a claim is provided as Appendix B.

An event that cannot be identified in this listing does not entitle the Contractor to make a claim under the Contract and hence will not be considered by the Engineer.

Events that do not give rise to an entitlement to claim under the Contract may yet be subject to consideration under the laws of the country where the contract is executed.

A frequently occurring example of an extra-contractual event that may be subject to adjustment by legal process is the consequence arising from an extraordinary increase in the price of a key material (e.g. bitumen, reinforcing steel) for which there is no remedial provision in the Contract (refer to Sub-Clause 13.7 and/or 13.8). The laws of the country may allow that such extraordinary increases were without the reasonable expectations of the Parties at the Base Date. Legal advice should be promptly obtained.

Claims for both additional payment and for the extensions of time follow the same procedural rules.

The Contractor's Representative should ensure that the following procedures are adopted:

- The event or circumstance giving rise to an entitlement to claim under the Contract has firstly to be identified by reference to the appropriate clause of the Contract.
- The Contractor is required to give notice of his claim for an extension of time, for additional payment or for both in writing no later than 28 days after the Contractor became aware or should have become aware of the event or circumstance. This giving notice of claim within the prescribed time limit of 28 days is vital to the Contractor's interests. The Contractor will forfeit his right to claim if he fails to submit his claim notice within the 28-day time limit. Exceptionally, in respect of Sub-Clause 4.12 'Unforeseeable Physical Conditions', notice has to be given as soon as practicable.
- A descriptive title for the claim notice should be selected and used on all future correspondence. A unique number could also be added for brevity and easy identification. This procedure will facilitate future document control, should the claim only be settled by use of DAB or arbitration procedures.
- The initial notice can be very brief giving only the essential facts of the event or circumstance, but importantly should contain the correct contractual references that permit the claim to be made and evaluated.
- Significant claim notifications may arise as a consequence of site instructions issued by the Engineer (particularly those instructions whose

ramifications are not readily appreciated). Often these instructions could be readily processed as a Variation in accordance with Clause 13 'Variations and Adjustments'. It is recommended that the Contractor's Representative discuss these issues directly with the Engineer. It is possible that the Engineer will agree to regulate the situation without the Contractor having to formally give notice of claim. However, it is equally possible that the Employer may have placed restrictions on the powers of the Engineer to deal expeditiously with Variations, so that the 28-day notice period for claims may be endangered.

- The notice can be very brief giving only the essential facts of the event or circumstance, but should contain the correct contractual references. If time is limited or if there remains uncertainty of the validity of the claim, or if the Engineer cannot provide an approved Variation in good time, then the Contractor should give notice of claim regardless of any other considerations. It is easy to withdraw a claim notice, but difficult to introduce a claim outside the 28-day time limit.

- The Contractor's Representative should give instructions to site staff to keep records where appropriate. Invite the Engineer to participate in all record-keeping.

- Having given notice of claim, the Contractor has to provide a fully detailed claim within 42 days of the Contractor becoming aware (or should have been aware) of the event or circumstance giving rise to the claim. Effectively, this gives an additional 14 days over and above the 28-day period provided for giving notice.

- It is important that the Contractor commences as quickly as possible with the preparation of the fully detailed claim. The FIDIC Conditions of Contract do not penalise the Contractor if he fails to comply with the 42-day provision, but it is in the Contractor's own interests to progress with the claim as quickly as possible. If more time is required, then the matter should be discussed with the Engineer in order to establish a longer time period.

- The claim presentation noted above is interim only and further submissions may be required. The quantification may require continuous updates should the event or circumstance continue.

- The Engineer may request that further details be provided. The Contractor should respond as quickly as possible.

- A consolidated claims' listing is to form part of the monthly Progress Report identified in Sub-Clause 4.21.

Appendices

Appendix A
Contractor's claims under a CONS contract

Sub-Clause	Title	Money	Time
1.9	Delayed Drawings or Instructions	x	x
2.1	Right of Access to the Site	x	x
4.7	Setting out (errors)	x	x
4.12	Unforeseen Physical Conditions	x(c)	x
4.24	Fossils	x(c)	x
7.4	Testing	x	x
8.4	Extension of Time for Completion	–	x
8.5	Delay Caused by Authorities	–	x
8.9	Consequences of Suspension	x(c)	x
10.2	Taking Over of Part of Works	x	–
10.3	Interference with Tests on Completion	x	x
11.8	Contractor to Search	x	x
12.4	Omissions (by Variation)	x(c)	–
13.2	Value Engineering	x	–
13.7	Changes in Legislation	x(c)	x
14.8	Delayed Payment	x(c)	–
16.1	Contractor's Entitlement to Suspend	x	x
16.4	Payment on Termination	x	–
17.1	Indemnities (by Employer)	x(c)	–
17.4	Consequences of Employer's Risks	x	x
18.1	General Requirement for Insurances (if supplied by Employer)	x(c)	–
19.4	Consequences of Force Majeure	x	x
19.6	Optional Payment Termination	x	–
20.1	Contractor's Claims (procedural)	x	x

A Contractor's Guide to the FIDIC Conditions of Contract, First Edition. Michael D. Robinson.
© 2011 John Wiley & Sons, Ltd. Published 2011 by John Wiley & Sons, Ltd.

Appendix A

Note

In most cases a Contractor can claim cost and a reasonable profit. However, for some items he can only claim 'cost'. These items are marked (c) in the above table.

Appendix B
Employer's claims under a CONS contract

Sub-Clause	Title
4.18	Electricity, Water, Gas if stated in the Contract
4.19	Employer's Equipment and Free-Issue Material
7.5	Rejection (Defective Plant and Materials)
7.6	Remedial Work (Contractor fails to carry out)
8.6	Rate of Progress (Contractor adopts revised methods that cause Employer additional cost)
8.7	Delay Damages (Contractor fails to complete on time)
9.4	Failure to pass tests on completion (Only if Employer incurs additional costs)
11.4	Failure to rectify defects (Contractor fails to rectify)
13.7	Adjustments for changes in Legislation (Reductions in cost to be refunded to Employer)
15.3	Valuation at Date of Termination (Contractor's property valued by Employer on Termination)
15.4	Payment after Termination (Employer may claim losses and damage after Termination)
17.1	Indemnities (Employer claims costs of events for which he is indemnified by Contractor)
18.1	General Requirements for Insurances (Employer makes claim if Contractor fails to insure)
18.2	Insurance for Works and Contractor's Equipment (Employer can claim refund if Contractor is unable to insure in accordance with Contract)

A Contractor's Guide to the FIDIC Conditions of Contract, First Edition. Michael D. Robinson.
© 2011 John Wiley & Sons, Ltd. Published 2011 by John Wiley & Sons, Ltd.

Appendix B

Appendix C
Conditions of Contract for Plant and Design-build (P & DB) – 'The Yellow Book'

The P & DB Conditions of Contract are intended for use where the Contractor designs and provides, in accordance with the Employer's requirements, fully functional plant or other works which may include architectural, civil, mechanical, electrical or other works.

The Employer's requirements are intended to precisely define the scope of Works. Not only is the Contractor responsible for design of the Works, but he also carries significant responsibilities for the commissioning of the Works (including training of the Employer's staff). He will also be required to provide extensive documentation including as-built documents and operation manuals. In contrast to the CONS form of contract where the Works are valued by a process of admeasurement, the P & DB contracts are valued as a lump sum (the Accepted Contract Amount). Further breakdowns of this lump sum are necessary for the purposes of evaluation of monthly Applications for Interim Payment Certificates.

Except as noted above, a significant proportion of the procedures and operation of a P & DB contract is not dissimilar to that of a CONS contract.

Those clauses of the P & DB contract that are amended from CONS, primarily as a consequence of the Contractor's design responsibilities, are commented upon below.

Sub-Clause 1.5 – Priority of Documents

The Employer's Requirements are given a lesser status than both the General and Particular Conditions of Contract, but are superior to the Contractor's Proposal provided with his tender.

Sub-Clause 1.9 – Errors in the Employer's Requirements

The consequences of any oversight made by the Contractor in the preparation of the Contractor's Proposal are to the account of the Contractor. In order to present a claim under this heading, the Contractor is required to demonstrate that there was indeed an error in the Employer's Requirements.

A considerable responsibility falls on the estimating office who, in the event of doubt, should request clarification from the Engineer. Data collected from the site visit should be carefully stored for future reference.

A Contractor's Guide to the FIDIC Conditions of Contract, First Edition. Michael D. Robinson.
© 2011 John Wiley & Sons, Ltd. Published 2011 by John Wiley & Sons, Ltd.

Appendix C

Sub-Clause 4.6 – Cooperation

Not only is the Contractor responsible for his own construction activities on site, but he is also required to coordinate the activities of other contractors on site (if any). This may have consequences that need to be evaluated in the preparation of the Programme.

Clause 5.0 – Design

This clause sets out the Contractor's design obligations in detail.

Sub-Clause 5.3 – Contractor's Undertaking/Sub-Clause 5.4 – Technical Standards

The Contractor undertakes that the design and the execution of the Works will be in accordance with the laws of the country and the documents forming the Contract.

A number of countries require that the technical standards adopted, the design, the execution and eventual handover of the Works are all in conformity with the local laws. It is possible that the requirement may be in contradiction to information given, for example, in the Employer's Requirements where international standards or standards of another country may be specified. Often the laws of the country effectively reduce the powers of the FIDIC Engineer.

Where necessary the estimating office should clarify theses issues. The Contractor's Representative should be made aware of any potential difficulties.

Sub-Clause 5.5 – Training

Sub-Clause 5.6 – As-Built Drawings

Sub-Clause 5.7 – Operation and Maintenance Manuals

The preparation and execution of these three activities can be time-consuming, and adequate provision has to be made in the preparation of the Programme. Consideration should be given to the likely skill levels of those selected for training.

Sub-Clause 9.1 – Contractor's Obligations

The following Tests on Completion are specified:

- pre-commissioning tests (dry tests)
- commissioning tests (operational tests)
- trial operation (group or full-load tests)

The Contractor is required to give the Engineer 21 days' notice of the intended date of executing these tests. This may have a linkage to the training programme. Appropriate allowance is to be made in the preparation of the Programme. It may be assumed that these tests are to be carried out before any Taking Over.

Sub-Clause 11.2 – Cost of Remedying Defects

Sub-Clause 11.2(c) states that the Contactor is responsible for improper operation or maintenance prior to the expiry date of the Defects Notification Period for the Works (or Section). This sub-clause refers to Sub-Clauses 5.5–5.7 (see above). It appears that the Contractor has a duty to comply with the requirements of Sub-Clauses 5.5–5.7, otherwise he runs the risk of being held responsible for faulty operation or maintenance by the Employer (or his Agents).

Sub-Clause 12.0 – Tests on Completion

Refer to summary quoted in Sub-Clause 9.1. This sub-clause deals with the execution of the Tests on Completion and with the remedies available to one Party in the event of failure of the other Party to comply.

Sub-Clause 13.1

The detailed definition of a Variation given in CONS is replaced with a simple statement that either the Engineer or the Contractor can initiate a Variation (without any detailed definition).

Sub-Clause 14.1 – The Contract Price

The Contract Price shall be the lump sum Accepted Contract Amount and subject to adjustments in accordance with the Contract. The Works completed are not required to be remeasured and evaluated.

Sub-Clause 14.4 – Schedule of Payment

The Accepted Contract Price (lump sum) may be broken down into smaller amounts in the tender. It is likely that the Contractor may be requested to break down the Accepted Contract Price into even smaller amounts to facilitate the value of completed works to be included in the Application for Interim Payment Certificates.

Appendix D
Conditions of Contract for EPC/Turnkey projects (EPCT) – 'The Silver Book'

These Conditions of Contract are intended for use where one entity (the Contractor) provides a fully equipped facility ready for operation at the 'turn of the key'. The Employer is required to provide a fully descriptive document specifying precisely what is to be built and to what standards. In defining the Employer's Requirements, he may provide preliminary drawings, site data, technical requirements including specifications. The Employer's Requirements may also contain requirements for specified outputs from the completed facility.

This form of Conditions of Contract has not found favour in the construction industry. The risk both for time and money that is allocated to the Contractor by the Silver Book is far greater than that allocated by the Yellow Book. The influential European Contractors' Association has declined to recommend the use of the Silver Book forms to its members, principally because it is considered that the high level of risk allocated to the Contractor is commercially unacceptable. Generally, there is a lack of reporting on any contracts that might be using the Silver Book forms.

The increasing use of Design, Build and Operate (DBO) projects (refer to discussion in Appendix E following) and the issue by FIDIC in 2008 of the Conditions of Contract for Design, Build and Operate projects (the 'Gold Book') have effectively eliminated one key type of project where the Silver Book might have been considered for use as a source document.

A Contractor's Guide to the FIDIC Conditions of Contract, First Edition. Michael D. Robinson.
© 2011 John Wiley & Sons, Ltd. Published 2011 by John Wiley & Sons, Ltd.

Appendix D

Appendix E
Other FIDIC publications

1. Short Form of Contract (the 'Green Book')

In addition to the Red Book, the Yellow Book and the Silver Book already discussed, the Green Book completes the 'Rainbow' suite of contract forms issued by FIDIC in 1999. The Green Book is intended for engineering and building work with low value. The work is to be simple and repetitive with little or no input from specialists or subcontractors. Exceptionally, the format of this contract form is concise and does not follow the pattern of the other contract forms of the Rainbow suite.

2. Conditions of Contract for Construction designed by the Employer for bank-financed projects only (the 'Pink Book')

Increasingly Multilateral Development Banks such as the World Bank, the European Bank for Reconstruction and Development, African Development Bank and others have become concerned at the high levels of corruption and misuse of funding provided by them. Originally these Multilateral Development Banks were of a mind to develop their own forms of contract which would incorporate provisions for the tighter control of funding and thereby eliminate potential corrupt practices.

Eventually the banks and FIDIC cooperated to provide a form of contract that would fulfil the need of the banks and yet retain the standard FIDIC features which are familiar to those engaged in the international construction industry.

The Pink Book is essentially a variant of the Red Book, wherein a number of clauses specifically relating to payment, control of money and similar topics have been added to the Red Book. Those familiar with the use of the Red Book will find little difficulty in the use of the Pink Book.

3. Conditions of Contract for Design, Build and Operate Projects (the 'Gold Book')

The Gold Book brings together the functions of design, construction, operation and maintenance of a facility into one contract and is intended for 'Design, Build and Operate' projects, usually abbreviated to DBO projects. The commissioning of a project is followed by an operation and maintenance period of 20 years (which may be varied). In that period the Contractor must meet stated operational targets and then hand back the project to the Employer at the end of the period in a pre-agreed condition.

A Contractor's Guide to the FIDIC Conditions of Contract, First Edition. Michael D. Robinson.
© 2011 John Wiley & Sons, Ltd. Published 2011 by John Wiley & Sons, Ltd.

Appendix E

Such major projects will be usually undertaken by large consortia, the partners of which provide their own individual skills to the consortia (design, build, operation and maintenance). Collectively referred to as the 'Concessionaire', the individual partners will perform their specific allocated tasks as subcontractors to the Concessionaire. In recent years this form of contract has found favour with public authorities because the financing has to be arranged by the Contractor through the major banks. The total cost of the project may be recovered by tolls and fees but it is possible that there will be some injection of public funds under certain conditions.

A regular user of the other standard FIDIC forms should have little difficulty in the use of this Gold Book.

4. Dredgers Contract (the 'Blue Book')

The Blue Book is intended for dredging and reclamation work that is designed by the Engineer.

5. Subcontract Forms

The previous Red Book entitled 'Conditions of Contract for Works of Civil Engineering Construction' (4th Edition 1992) was accompanied by a separate but complementary set of forms relating to subcontracts. Both were effectively superseded by the issue in 1999 of the new Red Book 'Conditions of Contract for Construction'. However, there was no issue of new complementary forms of subcontracts. Test editions of the revised subcontract forms were eventually issued in 2009 and it is likely that these forms will be issued in their final format in the near future.

Appendix F
Model form for submissions to the Engineer for approval and/or consent

PROJECT   Serial No.

ENGINEER: (Name)

CONTRACTOR: (Name)

SUBMITTAL TO THE ENGINEER FOR APPROVAL/CONSENT/INFORMATION

SUBJECT: Drawings/Method Statement/Material Samples/Test Results/Plant
           Acquisition/Q.A. Report/Programmes/Health and Safety   (Identify One)

TITLE: (Specify Title)

DETAIL: Drawing No./Document No./Sample/Other

CLAUSE(S):   ....

REF No.:   ....

ATTACHMENTS: ....

               ....

DISTRIBUTION:

Submitted by .... Contractor	Resubmittal required .... Engineer
Date:	Date: ....
Resubmittal by .... Contractor	Approved subject to corrections as noted .... Engineer
OTHER:	Approval/Consent .... Engineer
	Date: ....

A Contractor's Guide to the FIDIC Conditions of Contract, First Edition. Michael D. Robinson.
© 2011 John Wiley & Sons, Ltd. Published 2011 by John Wiley & Sons, Ltd.

Appendix G
Model form of daywork/daily record sheets

Sub-Clause 13.6 'Daywork' requires the Contractor to submit details of resources utilised on a daily basis to the Engineer for his confirmatory signature.

Additionally, there are many instances in the Contract where the keeping (and agreement) of daily records is crucial if the Contractor is to be properly reimbursed for his efforts. This applies particularly to those events where the Contractor is entitled to payment of cost. Further, there will be other occasions, particularly relating to claims and their quantification, where accurate records of actual events would be beneficial.

Below is a proposed standard format which can be varied to suit the requirements of an individual site. These daywork/daily record sheets should be colour-printed in groups of five and bound in sets of 100 (20 × 5).

Each set of five would have a unique sequential number. This would help identify records that are not signed, not presented or simply 'lost' in the system.

The top copy and one other would be taken by the Engineer and the next two copies by the Contractor's site office. These four copies would be perforated for separation. A fifth copy, unperforated, would be kept in the Contractor's field office responsible for producing the record sheets.

It may happen that the Contractor's supervisory staff are not fluent in the language of the Contract. Provided that Badge No./Fleet No./Material Codes are correctly recorded, together with the relevant quantities, the form can be conveniently completed by a junior staff member with the correct language skills.

The valuation of the individual sheets takes place in the Contractor's site office. The quantum, whether for daywork or other purposes, can be sent to the Engineer as part of the monthly Application for Interim Certificate or as part of a claim presentation accompanied by a copy of the original, signed daywork/daily record sheet.

A Contractor's Guide to the FIDIC Conditions of Contract, First Edition. Michael D. Robinson.
© 2011 John Wiley & Sons, Ltd. Published 2011 by John Wiley & Sons, Ltd.

Appendix G

Date   DAYWORK/DAILY RECORD SHEET   Sheet Reference

....

PROJECT .... SECTION ....

DESCRIPTION..

REFERENCE (if any)...

LABOUR					EQUIPMENT				MATERIALS			
	Badge	Name	Trade	Hours		Fleet No.	Description	Hours		Code	Description	Quantity	Unit
1					1				1				
2					2				2				
3					3				3				
4					4				4				
5					5				5				
6					6				6				
7					7				7				
8					8				8				
9					9				9				
10					10				10				
11					11				11				

CONTRACTOR: ....   ENGINEER:.......................

Distribution:	Engineer:	white + yellow
	Contractor's Office:	green + pink
	Site:	blue – fast copy

Appendix H
Evaluation of cost

There are a number of events and circumstances described in the FIDIC Conditions of Contract that entitle the Contractor to claim reimbursement of his costs. These events and circumstances are summarised in Appendix A.

Cost is defined in Sub-Clause 1.1.4.3 of the Conditions of Contract as '... all expenditure reasonably incurred ... including overheads ... but does not include profit'. Unfortunately, this brief definition does not provide meaningful guidance in respect of the potential complexities inherent in the calculation of Cost.

In order to demonstrate Cost with exactitude, the Contractor would be required to maintain detailed records of all of his operations relating to the event or circumstance giving rise to his cost claim. The principal difficulties are not necessarily the agreement of work hours or the quantity of resources employed, but the determination of the unit cost of those resources and the calculation of overheads (without profit). Further, the cost of maintaining site records and analysing the data may be prohibitive and out of proportion to the value of the claim.

Clearly, it is impractical for the Contractor to maintain detailed records of every aspect of the work performed for inclusion in a quantification of a cost claim, and equally it is impractical for the Engineer to verify those records. The problem is exacerbated by the probability that the event or circumstance under evaluation will share resources with other activities that are not the subject of claim. The division of the cost of those shared resources will be difficult to achieve in a conclusive manner. Smaller contracting companies undertaking smaller projects are less likely to have the resources and expertise to operate a major costing programme. Consequently, for these smaller projects, particularly in less-developed countries, where support is less readily available, it is unavoidable that other methods of valuing cost claims are considered.

It has been the author's experience, in the circumstances described above, that 'cost' is frequently artificially developed by reference to appropriate items in the Bill of Quantities (or occasionally Daywork rates) in much the same manner as for the valuation of a Variation with an appropriate notional deduction for profit. A further deduction may be due in respect of the fixed-cost element of the total overhead (refer to Appendix I for discussion on the subject of Contractor's Overheads). This process of approximating cost is frequently adopted by insurance companies when dealing with a construction claim.

Appendix A lists eight sub-clauses identifying those events and circumstances that entitle the Contractor to seek reimbursement of his costs. Of particular significance are claims made under the provisions of Sub-Clause

Appendix H

4.12 'Unforeseeable Physical Conditions' which, if proven, entitle the Contractor to '… payment of any … cost'.

Claims presented under this heading are frequently complex and difficult to prepare and present in a concise, professional manner. The additional requirement to prepare a quantification based on cost records can be difficult for the reasons highlighted above.

For larger projects, which are likely to be performed by larger, better-resourced and more sophisticated contracting companies, it is quite probable that they will have a dedicated on-site department who are able to provide a useful amount of cost data to support a cost-claim valuation. The staff of the Engineer remain with the difficulty of verifying the Contractor's data.

The author has experience of a very large dam project which was badly damaged by a series of unforeseen events. The cost of repairing the damage was estimated to be in excess of US$ 100 million at 1974 prices. The repair work took almost two years to complete and was executed in parallel with other contract work of a similar value. The repair work was the subject of an insurance claim to be paid at cost, whilst the contract work continued to be paid in accordance with the terms and conditions of the Contract.

Part of the Contractor's resources was exclusively allocated to the repair works and a further part exclusively to the contracted work. However, a significant element of the total available resources was shared between the two operations in a random manner according to priorities set by the Contractor's management and agreed by the Engineer (batch plants, work-shops, offices, accommodation etc.).

The Employer, the Contractor and the Insurer agreed to keep detailed records of all operations on the site, to develop costings of each operation and to sub-divide the total costs into those attributable to the repair works (and the subject of an insurance claim) and those attributable to the contract works. To achieve this, the Employer and the Contractor also agreed – with the knowledge of the Insurer – that an independent, specialist team accept-able to both Parties should be brought to site to supplement the Contractor's own cost department with the task of directing this record-keeping and evaluation. To the credit of both Parties, it was agreed in advance that the conclusions of the independent specialists would be accepted without reser-vation. This was important because if the Insurer declined acceptance of the claim, then either the Employer or the Contractor would assume responsibil-ity for the costs incurred. After three years of effort the insurance claim was finalised and presented. Other works continued to be measured and evalu-ated in accordance with the terms and conditions of the Contract.

Although this was indeed an extreme case, it serves to demonstrate the difference in approach to resolving cost issues on large projects from that required for smaller projects discussed earlier in this Appendix.

Appendix I
Contractor's overhead costs

1.

The use of the terms 'overhead' and 'overhead costs' is spread throughout the FIDIC Conditions of Contract and in the explanatory text of the FIDIC Guide without there being a corresponding definition included in Sub-Clause 1.1 'Definitions'. Overhead costs may be defined as those expenses that together with taxes and planned profit are not directly chargeable to the cost of production. Production costs, principally the cost of the plant, labour and materials, are conventionally referred to as direct costs. Thus, the summation of overhead costs and direct costs represents the total cost of a given project to the Contractor. Occasionally, in other literature, the reader may find reference to 'indirect costs' in substitution for 'overhead costs'. For consistency, this book follows the FIDIC preference for the use of 'overhead costs'.

2.

In order to maintain commercial confidentiality, access to the Contractor's tender summary sheet or so-called 'top sheet' is normally restricted to a limited number of the Contractor's senior management.

Nonetheless, it seems inevitable that at some point essential pricing data will have to be made available to the Engineer in order to facilitate the valuation of variations, claim valuation and settlement, particularly those claims related to extension of time.

It has been the author's experience that it is preferable that the principal features of the Contractor's 'top sheet' are presented to, and accepted by, the Employer/Engineer at an early stage of the Contract and before claims and disputes arise. It becomes increasingly difficult to reach a general agreement on the value of overheads after claims or disputes have arisen, particularly if the Engineer's relevant site staff have inadequate understanding of the principles used in the compilation of the Contractor's 'top sheet'.

The Contractor's 'top sheet' is prepared by his estimating office and should be adjusted prior to commencement of the Works to reflect the consequences of agreements reached in any post-tender meetings with the Employer.

A Contractor's Guide to the FIDIC Conditions of Contract, First Edition. Michael D. Robinson.
© 2011 John Wiley & Sons, Ltd. Published 2011 by John Wiley & Sons, Ltd.

3.

Conventionally, the Contractor's overhead costs are expressed as a percentage of direct costs even though the Contractor's estimating office will, for the most part, have calculated the various elements of the overhead costs as individual sums of money. This percentage can vary considerably from more than 40% on a large isolated project (where the Contractor has to provide a large amount of facilities and services, e.g. housing, schools, hospitals etc.) to less than 20% on a small project in a developed location, where site establishment is minimal and full use is made of local suppliers and services.

The Contractor's overhead costs may be reduced if some of these costs are paid directly by means of specific bill items in the Bill of Quantities.

4.

A proportion of the overhead will be incurred off site ('Head Office Expenses') and the remainder on the site ('Site Office Expenses'). Both the Head Office Expenses and the Site Office Expenses can be further sub-divided into time-related costs and fixed-overhead costs.

The Contractor's 'top sheet' will typically contain the following information:

Direct Costs	%	%
Equipment	30	
Labour	25	
Materials	25	
Subcontractors	<u>20</u>	100
Head Office Expenses		
Time-Related Overhead Costs	4	
Fixed-Overhead Costs	<u>2</u>	6
Site Office Expenses		
Time-Related Overhead Costs		
• expatriatestaff		
• non-productive local staff		
• officevehicles		
• officemaintenance		
• consumables		
• communications	9	
Fixed-Overhead Costs		
• provideofficesetc	5	
• establishmentdemobilizationcosts	<u>2</u>	16
<u>Total Costs</u>		122
<u>Profit, Risk, Financing (6% of total cost)</u>	<u>7.32</u>	<u>7.32</u>
Total Selling Price		<u>129.32</u>
(Accepted Contract Amount)		

The breakdown of the Accepted Contract Amount demonstrated above is an important aid in the following matters:

(a)   the agreement of new rates for changes in quantities of work to be performed (Sub-Clause 12.3(a) refers)
(b)   the agreement of new rates for works that are the subject of a Variation (Sub-Clause 12.3(b) refers)
(c)   the evaluation of financial claims arising from any award of an Extension of Time for Completion (Clause 8.4 refers). As summarised in Appendix A, there are fourteen in number of events or circumstances that permit the Contractor to claim additional payment in respect of Extension of Time for Completion. Of those fourteen instances, four restrict the Contractor's entitlement to his costs only.

In the administration of those matters summarised above, there is a general assumption that Overhead Costs are spread evenly over all bill items and over the full period of the Contract. In particular, Variations made under the provisions of Sub-Clause 12.3 are most likely to be evaluated on this assumption. For the reasons highlighted in Appendix H, it is impractical to assess the individual overhead applicable to individual bill items, and the use of a global average percentage for all items is seemingly inevitable, excluding only those items where specific alternative measures are provided (e.g. the percentage for adjustment of Provisional Sums – Sub-Clause 13.5(b) refers).

Referring to the breakdown given in the previous page, it can be stated as a generalisation that a fixed overhead of 29.32% would be applicable to all new evaluations made under the provisions summarised in (a), (b) and (c) above, excluding items where the evaluation is specified to be based on cost only.

Nonetheless, there are occasions when the practice of averaging overheads over the period of the Contract is not appropriate. The reality is that the Contractor does not incur his Overhead Costs evenly over the period of the Contract.

Mobilisation Period
In the initial stages of a Contract it takes time for the Contractor to mobilise his resources and establish himself on Site. His expenditure on Fixed-Overhead Costs will be relatively high and Time-Related Costs will gradually increase over this period as more and more operations are commenced.

Construction Period
Once the mobilisation period is completed, expenditure on Fixed Overheads can be assumed to fall to a relatively constant level for the construction period. Equally, Time-Related Costs can also be assumed to fall to a relatively constant level, although this depends considerably on the incidence of high-value work items. These Time-Related Costs will eventually reduce as the date for Taking Over approaches, when sections of the Works are completed and the Contractor's resources are reduced.

Defects Liability Period
Fixed-Overhead Costs will chiefly derive from the final demobilisation of the Contractor's resources. Time-Related Costs will relate to completion

of outstanding works and the correction of defects, which under average circumstances will be largely complete within the first few months of the Defects Liability Period.

If no specific cost data is available, the incidence of expenditure for all Overhead Costs may be estimated from other documents, including the Contractor's cash-flow projections and the Programme of Works.

Fixed-Overhead Costs

Provided that the final value of the measured works is at least equal to the Accepted Contract Value, then the Contractor will recover his Fixed-Overhead Costs in full, and no further payment is due in respect of any period of excusable delay. Should special circumstances cause the Contractor to incur disproportionate additional Fixed-Overhead Costs, then these costs are to be separately identified and evaluated for inclusion in the relevant Contractor's claim.

Time-Related Costs

A number of differing scenarios are possible:

Case (a)
Should the whole of the Works be delayed or suspended, then the Contractor is entitled to recover in full the amount of Time-Related Costs incurred in the period of delay. Consequently, the amount due will vary according to the timing of the delay in the construction cycle.

Case (b)
An excusable delay occurs which lies on the critical path to completion. Work continues on other non-critical activities. In such circumstances, the Contractor is entitled to claim the full amount of the Time-Related Overheads as for Case (a), but will be required to adjust that amount proportionately to the contribution received from the payment for the works not affected by the delay.

Case (c)
An excusable delay of three months lies on the critical path to completion. However, the Contractor is responsible for a parallel non-critical delay of two months.
The Contractor is entitled to an extension of time for the full period of the total three months' delay. However, this entitlement to payment of additional Time-Related Costs will be restricted to (three months minus two months), i.e. one month net.
The Contractor would also be justified in requesting payment of Time-Related Overheads for the parallel two months' delay period. In a similar manner to that described in Case (a) above, he would be expected to make an adjustment to his request for payment proportionately to the notional

contribution he would have received in respect of the part of the Works delayed by him.

The above scenarios give only general guidelines. The Contractor's entitlement will depend on actual events and circumstances that give rise to the claim and to the detailed wording of the Contract Documents.

Appendix J
Model letters for use by the Contractor

Letter to the Engineer   c.c. Employer   ML 1.3

Sub-Clause – 1.3 Communications

We confirm the agreement made between us on (date) in respect of site communications.

Communications between us shall be:

(1) In writing and delivered by hand (against receipt) or
(2) By mail or courier or
(3) By facsimile or
(4) By e-mail. Hard copies of all e-mails to be provided within 3 days of the date of the e-mail by alternatives (1) or (2) above.

All communications will be signed by the undersigned (one or two signatories?). (Name) is an authorised alternative signatory.

Yours etc.

A Contractor's Guide to the FIDIC Conditions of Contract, First Edition. Michael D. Robinson.
© 2011 John Wiley & Sons, Ltd. Published 2011 by John Wiley & Sons, Ltd.

Letter to the Engineer   ML 1.8

Sub-Clause 1.8 – Supply of Documents

In accordance with the provisions of Sub-Clause 1.8, please provide us with two copies of the Contract Documents (Specification and Drawings). The Documents are to be those intended for construction purposes.

Yours etc.

Note: 1.   The Contract Documents are due to be supplied by the Engineer and not the Employer.
        2.   Query whether the Contract Documents are available in electronic format.

Letter to the Engineer   ML 1.9

Sub-Clause 1.9 – Request for Drawings and Instructions

In accordance with the provisions of Sub-Clause 1.9, we hereby request you to
provide us with:

Alt. 1   Drawings for (give details).In accordance with the programme, we require
these drawings no later than (Date).

Alt. 2   (a)   Clarification of the following anomaly (describe the anomaly).
         (b)   Instructions for (describe instructions that are now requested and
               when they are required).

Yours etc.

Letter to the Employer   c.c. Engineer   ML 2.1a

Sub-Clause 2.1 – Access to Site

By letter (reference – date) the Engineer has instructed us that the Commencement Date shall be (date).

In accordance with Sub-Clause 2.1, we hereby request you to provide us with Access to the Site in accordance with the following schedule:

(The Schedule should be for all of the site or sections or parts. The Schedule is to be compatible with the Programme.).

We request that the site (or part) be formally inspected at the date when access is provided.

Yours etc.

Letter to the Engineer   c.c. Employer   ML 2.1b

<u>Claim No. *</u>
<u>Sub-Clause 2.1 – Access to Site</u>
<u>Delayed Access to Site</u>

Following receipt of your notice of commencement (reference and date), we requested the Employer, by our letter (reference and date) , to provide us with access to site (modify as necessary for parts or sections) all in accordance with the provisions of Sub-Clause 2.1. At the date of this letter we have not been granted the requested access and the Works cannot be commenced.

In accordance with the provisions of Sub-Clause 2.1 and in compliance with Sub-Clauses 8.4 and 20.1, we hereby notify you that we consider ourselves entitled to an extension of time with respect to the delay, together with reimbursement of our costs plus reasonable profit.

Yours etc.

Note: If the access was provided late, the second paragraph can be modified to give the actual date when access was provided and the precise number of days of delay.

Letter to the Engineer   c.c. Employer   ML 2.1c

<u>Claim No.</u> *
<u>Sub-Clause 2.1 – Access to Site</u>
<u>Delayed Access to Site</u>

Following receipt of your notice of commencement (reference and date), we requested that the Employer provide us with access to the site (modify as necessary for parts or sections) all in accordance with the provisions of Sub-Clause 2.1.

On (date) we were offered possession of the site (modify as necessary for parts or sections) (give details). However, the site was

(1)   occupied by others
(2)   contaminated with debris not present at the Base Date
(3)   inaccessible due to access being denied by others (typically expropriation or other authorities)
(4)   other

The nature of the obstructions noted above are such as will not permit us to enter the site (modify as necessary for parts or sections) and to work as planned. We therefore decline to enter the site until the situation is rectified.

Please consult the Employer and advise us how unrestricted access will be provided to us. Should we be instructed or requested to provide access, we shall do so on receipt of your instructions and we will require additional payment, the detail of which is to be agreed.

In accordance with the provisions of Sub-Clause 2.1 and in compliance with Sub-Clauses 8.4 and 20.1, we hereby notify you that we consider ourselves entitled to an extension of time with respect to this delay in providing access to the site, together with reimbursement of our costs plus reasonable profit.

Yours etc.

Letter to the Engineer   c.c. Employer   ML 2.1d

Claim No. *
Sub-Clause 2.1 – Access to Site
Interference with Access to Site

Following receipt of your notice of commencement (reference and date), we requested that the Employer provide us with access to the site (modify as necessary for parts and sections) all in accordance with the provisions of Sub-Clause 2.1.

On (date) we were offered possession of the site (modify as necessary for parts and sections) (give details). However, the site was:

(1) occupied by others
(2) contaminated with debris not present at Base Date
(3) inaccessible due to access being denied by others (typically expropriation)
(4) other

The nature of these obstructions is such that it is not possible to commence work in (describe area/section not available).

We have been instructed (give reference) to commence work in alternative (area/section) in contradiction to the agreed Programme of Work.

(If appropriate add the following:)

This change in planning will disrupt our activities (explain why – additional travel time, lower productivity etc.). Our site activities will be delayed and disrupted with reduced productivity and higher unit costs.

In accordance with the provisions of Sub-Clause 2.1 and in compliance with Sub-Clauses 8.4 and 20.1, we hereby notify you that we consider ourselves entitled to an extension of time with respect to this delay in providing the required access to the site, together with reimbursement of our costs plus reasonable profit.

Yours etc.

Letter to the Employer   c.c. Engineer   ML 2.2

Sub-Clause 2.2 – Permits, Licences or Approval

We request your kind assistance in dealing with the following matter.

(Describe the problem for which the Employer's assistance is requested. In addition to help in locating official or legal documents, it is probable that assistance may be required in dealing with government bodies or statutory authorities.)

Yours etc.

Letter to the Employer   c.c. Engineer   ML 2.4

<u>Sub-Clause 2.4 – Employer's Financial Arrangements</u>

(This is a rare occurrence and has to be approached sensitively, possibly preceded by discussions at a high level.)

We wish to advise you that we have re-evaluated the likely final Contract Price including the value of claims and other unresolved items, and including the value of additional works indicated to us by the Engineer.

The details are given in an attachment to this letter.

The indications are that the original Contract Price will be significantly exceeded.

Please would you confirm to us that sufficient funding is available/or will become available to cover these additional costs.

Yours etc.

Letter to the Engineer   c.c. Employer   ML 2.5

Sub-Clause 2.5 – Employer's Claims

(The most likely cause of the Employer making a claim is non-excusable delay in completion by the Contractor, leading to the imposition of Delay Damages.)

We have received a copy of the Employer's letter (date, reference) in which the Employer states entitlement to delay damages on account of non-excusable delays by the Contractor in completing the Works.

We wish to point out that we have registered a significant number of claims which we consider properly entitle us to (further) extensions of time in which to complete the Works. Details are attached.

In considering the Employer's claim, it is required that prior to issuing your determination you adjudicate our claims and only then proceed with your determination in accordance with Sub-Clause 3.5.

Yours etc.

Letter to the Engineer   c.c. Employer   ML 3.2

Sub-Clause 3.2 – Delegation by the Engineer

In accordance with the provisions of Sub-Clause 3.2, please inform us which of your duties and authority you have delegated to the Engineer's Representative.

Additionally, please advise us what duties and authority are delegated to any assistants to the Engineer's Representative.

Yours etc.

Letter to the Engineer   c.c. Employer   ML 3.3a

Sub-Clause 3.3 – Instructions of the Engineer

We confirm having received your verbal instructions to (describe the nature of the instructions)

(and if appropriate)

We propose payment for the work contained in your instructions at the existing bill rates

(or)

Your instructions constitute a Variation to the Works and we shall separately provide our proposed method of payment.

Yours etc.

Letter to the Engineer   ML 3.3b

Sub-Clause 3.3 – Instructions of the Engineer

This sub-clause describes a 'duty' of the Engineer. The procedure for processing the Contractor's claims is described in Sub-Clause 20.1. No further submissions are required from the Contractor under the provisions of this sub-clause.

Letter to the Employer   c.c. Engineer   ML 4.2

Sub-Clause 4.2 – Performance Security

Please find attached the original of the Performance Security as specified by Sub-Clause 4.2.

Yours etc.

Letter to the Engineer   c.c. Employer   ML 4.3a

To be sent by the Contractor's Head Office

Sub-Clause 4.3 – Contractor's Representative

We formally confirm the appointment of (name as identified in a document of the Contract) as the Contractor's Representative. A copy of the curriculum vitae of (name) is attached for your records.

Yours etc.

(or)

ML 4.3b

We propose (name 1) as the Contractor's Representative in replacement of (name 2) named in the Tender Submission. (Name 2) is no longer available for this appointment.

The curriculum vitae of (name 1) is attached for your review. Please may we have your earliest consent to this appointment.

Yours etc.

Letter to the Engineer   c.c. Employer   ML 4.4

Sub-Clause 4.4 – Subcontractors

As detailed in our tender submission we confirm our intention to subcontract parts of the Works as follows:

                    Name of Subcontractor   Work subcontracted
1.
2.
3.

Copies of the documentation attached to the tender, supplemented where necessary, are attached for your information and records.

Yours etc.

(or)

We hereby request your consent to sublet the following part(s) of the Works to (name and address of subcontractor).

Works to be subcontracted: (give descriptive detail)

In support of this request we attach the following documentation:

1.
2.
3.

Yours etc.

Letter to the Engineer   ML 4.7a

Sub-Clause – 4.7 Setting Out

We are in receipt of setting-out data for the Works provided to us on (date). In using this data, we have set out the Works and have noted the following errors (description required) in the data.

Please issue us with corrective instructions as soon as possible.

Yours etc.

(or)

Letter to the Engineer   ML 4.7b

Claim No. *
Sub-Clause – 4.7 Setting Out
Consequence of Errors in Setting Out Data

By letter (reference and date) we advised you of errors in the setting-out data provided to us. The nature of the errors was such as could not have been foreseen by an experienced contractor.

We received your corrective instructions by your letter (reference and date), a delay of ... days.

In accordance with the provisions of Sub-Clause 4.7, we hereby notify you that we consider ourselves entitled to an extension of time of .... days, together with reimbursement of our costs plus reasonable profit.

Yours etc.

Letter to the Engineer   ML 4.8

<u>Sub-Clause 4.8 – Safety Procedures</u>

We attach hereto a copy of our standard Health and Safety Manual. This is supplemented by a further manual which modifies the standard document to meet the needs of this project.

Please advise us of any comments you may have.

Yours etc.

Letter to the Engineer   ML 4.9

Sub-Clause 4.9 – Quality Assurance

We attach hereto a copy of our manual detailing the quality-assurance system to be used to comply with the requirements of the Contract.

(If appropriate, add: The quality assurance system follows the recommendations of ISO 9001).

Supplementary documentation will be submitted as and when necessary.

Yours etc.

Letter to the Employer   c.c. Engineer   ML 4.10

Sub-Clause 4.10 – Site Data

Please advise us if you have acquired further Site Data since Base Date in respect of (give details of areas of interest or concern).

If further material is available, please provide two copies of the data at your earliest convenience.

Yours etc.

Letter to the Engineer   ML 4.12

Claim No. * (Provide descriptive title)
Sub-Clause 4.12 – Unforeseeable Physical Conditions

(Give a description of the event that is considered to represent an Unforeseeable Physical Condition. Make a statement to indicate if the Unforeseeable Physical Condition is ongoing or has ended. It is not necessary to provide all details in this first submission, but it is important to notify the Engineer of the event as soon as possible.)

We consider that the above event represents an Unforeseeable Physical Condition as described in Sub-Clause 4.12 and entitles us to an extension of time together with reimbursement of our costs (but not profit).

We are maintaining detailed records of our activities and request your cooperation in agreeing these records.

Yours etc.

Note: The above letter will require submission of a fully detailed claim within a further period of 28 days.

Letter to the Engineer   ML 4.16

<u>Sub-Clause 4.16 – Transport of Goods</u>
<u>Arrival on Site: (Describe the Goods)</u>

We write to advise you that the following Goods are expected to be delivered to site on (date) (or alternatively: in week No. *).

Yours etc.

Letter to the Engineer   ML 4.21a

Sub-Clause 4.21 – Progress Report
Proposed Template for Progress Reports

We enclose the proposed template to be used for Progress Reports. This template
follows the order of the listing given in Sub-Clause 4.21.

Your consent is requested.

Yours etc.

Letter to the Engineer   ML 4.21b

<u>Sub-Clause 4.21 – Progress Report</u>
<u>Progress Report No. * for (month/year)</u>

We enclose six copies of the above Progress Report.

Yours etc.

Letter to the Engineer   ML 4.24a

Sub-Clause 4.24 – Fossils
Discovery of (description) on Site

On (date) (description) was found on site at (location). Please urgently provide us with detailed instructions for protection and/or disposal of the same. (Alternatively, state that the item(s) have been taken into store (at location).)

Yours etc.

Letter to the Engineer   ML 4.24b

Claim No. *
Sub-Clause 4.24 – Fossils
Discovery of (description) on Site

On (date) (description) was found on site at (location). We received your instructions (reference, date) requiring us to suspend work pending further
instructions.

In accordance with the provisions of Sub-Clause 4.24, we hereby notify you that
we consider ourselves entitled to an extension of time together with reimbursement of our costs.

We are maintaining records of our activities and request your cooperation in
agreeing these records.

Yours etc.

Letter(s) to Nominated Subcontractors   ML 5.0

<u>Project Title</u>
<u>Submission of Documentation</u>

In accordance with the provisions of Sub-Clause 4.21 of the Main Contract, we are required to submit to the Engineer detailed Monthly Reports as a prerequisite to the issue of Interim Payment Certificates in accordance with Sub-Clause 14.6 of the Main Contract.

We now enclose for your further action a copy of the approved template for these Monthly Reports (including the format of the Application for Interim Payment Certificates described in Sub-Clause 14.3).

You are requested to ensure that your corresponding submissions provided to us conform to these templates and are prepared in such a manner as will facilitate incorporation into our own corresponding submissions under the Main Contract.

Yours etc.

Letter to the Engineer   ML 6.5

Sub-Clause 6.5 – Working Hours

We advise you that our working hours will be:

Office ....   (Monday – Friday)   ....   (Saturday)

Field Staff ....   (Monday – Friday)   ....   (Saturday)

Subject to the approval of the local authorities, we intend to work extended shifts for quarry operations, haulage (and other).

Occasionally our workshops may also work extended shifts for activities not connected with the permanent works and therefore do not require your supervision.

Yours etc.

Note: The key issue is whether the Working Hours are restricted. Even if the Working Hours can be extended, the Engineer may require the Contractor to pay the Engineer's staff costs. The Contractor's estimating office is required to minimise the risk at the date of tender.

Letter to the Engineer   ML 6.7

<u>Sub-Clause 6.7 – Health and Safety</u>
<u>Report of Accident on Site (Date)</u>

We regret to inform you of an accident which occurred on the project at (time) on (date). The incident was investigated by our Safety Officer, a copy of whose report is attached for your information.

(Optional) The relevant authorities have been informed.

Yours etc.

Note: The Safety Officer's report should contain recommendations for remedial action including further training etc.

Letter to the Engineer   ML 7.2

Sub-Clause 7.2 – Samples

(The Contractor is required to submit various samples to the Engineer for 'consent' – not 'approval' – unless stated elsewhere in the Contract.)

Each sample can be submitted under cover of a simple covering letter.

Many other items (programmes, method statements, test results etc.) have also to be submitted to the Engineer. Some projects, particularly those with architectural features, may require a large number of submissions which can be difficult to administer if not handled in a uniform manner.

Consequently, it is recommended that a standard format be adopted to facilitate document control. A sample format is provided in Appendix E.

Appendix J

Letter to the Engineer   ML 8.3

<u>Sub-Clause 8.3 – Programme</u>
<u>Submission of Programme</u>

We herewith attach a copy of our detailed time programme.

The programme is accompanied by the following documents: ....

(Refer to listing provided in Sub-Clause 8.3.)

Yours etc.

Note: Future delay events are also to be reported. Significant delay events can
          be reported in correspondence, including delays that are the subject of
          claims. Delays generally can be reported and recorded in the Progress
          Reports (Sub-Clause 4.21) and in Site Meetings.

Letter to the Engineer   ML 8.6

Sub-Clause 8.6 – Rate of Progress
Response to Engineer's Letter (reference, date)

With reference to your letter (reference, date), we are taking the following actions to make up for time lost due to inexcusable delays:

(a)
(b)
(c)

Note: This sub-clause refers only to inexcusable delays. Part of the total delay may be due to excusable delay which may not yet be evaluated by the Engineer. Additional wording may be required in order that the overall situation is clearly understood.

Letter to the Engineer   ML 8.9

<u>Claim No. *</u>
<u>Sub-Clause 8.9 – Consequences of Suspension</u>

We refer to your letter (reference, date) instructing us to suspend (all/part of) the Works.

In accordance with the provisions of Sub-Clause 8.9 and in compliance with the requirements of Sub-Clauses 8.4 and 20.1, we hereby notify you that we consider ourselves entitled to an extension of time with respect to delay, together with reimbursement of our costs.

We are maintaining records of our activities and request your cooperation in agreeing these records.

Yours etc.

Letter to the Engineer   ML 8.11a

<u>Sub-Clause 8.11 – Prolonged Suspension</u>
<u>Suspension of the Works</u>
<u>(If only part, give the part a title or description)</u>

We refer to your letter (reference, date) by which the Engineer issued a Suspension of the Works (if a part, describe the part) with effective date … (date).

The suspension now exceeds 84 days' duration and we now request your permission to proceed.

Yours etc.

Letter to the Engineer   ML 8.11b

<u>Sub-Clause 8.11 – Prolonged Suspension</u>
<u>Suspension of the Works</u>
<u>(If only part, give the part a title or description)</u>

We refer to your letter (reference, date) by which the Engineer issued a Suspension of the Works (if part, describe the part) with effective date (date). The period of suspension has exceeded 84 days and by our letter (reference, date) we requested permission to proceed.

After 28 days since making our request, we have not received permission to proceed.

Consequently, we give notice that we now consider the suspended part of the Works to be omitted from our scope of works.

(or)

Consequently, we give notice of termination for the whole of the works.

Yours etc.

Letter to the Engineer   ML 9.1

<u>Sub-Clause 9.1 – Tests on Completion</u>

We hereby give 21 days' notice of our intention to carry out the Tests on Completion in accordance with the following schedule:

1. Potable Water   on (date)
2. Power Supply H.T.   on (date)
3. Fire and Alarm Systems   on (date)

(The above are examples only.)

Yours etc.

Letter to the Engineer   ML 10.1a

<u>Sub-Clause 10.1 – Taking Over by the Employer</u>
<u>Application for Taking Over of the Whole of the Works</u>

In accordance with the provisions of Sub-Clause 10.1, we hereby give 14 days' notice that the whole of the Works will be complete and ready for taking over by the Employer on (date).

We request you to make arrangements with the Employer, so that he is prepared and ready to operate and safeguard the Works from the date of taking over.

Yours etc.

Note: 1.   The Contractor should continuously liaise with the Engineer prior to the sending of this letter, so that all potential objections are already dealt with.
        2.   In some jurisdictions taking over is achieved by committees appointed by the Employer in accordance with the local law. The taking over in such circumstances may be prolonged. The procedure is to be investigated well in advance of anticipated completion.

Letter to the Engineer   ML 10.1b

Sub-Clause 10.1 – Taking Over of a Section of the Works
(Describe briefly the section to be handed over)

(The taking over of a section of the Works to be handed over has to be so specified in the Contract, otherwise it becomes a part of the Works (refer to letter ML 10.1c below).)

In accordance with the provisions of Sub-Clause 10.1, we hereby give 14 days' notice that the above-described section of the Works will be complete and ready for taking over by the Employer on (date).

We request you to make arrangements with the Employer, so that he is prepared and ready to safeguard the Works from the date of taking over.

Yours etc.

Letter to the Engineer   ML 10.2

Sub-Clause 10.2 – Request for a Taking Over of Parts of the Works
(Describe briefly the part under reference)

(It may be mutually convenient to both Employer and Contractor for the Employer to take over a part of the Works, even though such taking over is not foreseen in the Contract documents. Such a situation may arise when the Employer has a need to use or allow others – such as the general public – to use the part of the Works.)

We refer to the various discussions concerning the taking over of the above part of the Works. The Employer has indicated a need to take over this part of the Works so that it may be brought into use.

Please obtain the consent of the Employer for you to issue a Taking Over Certificate for this part of the Works. This part of the Works will be available for taking over in 14 days of this letter/is available for immediate taking over.

Yours etc.

Letter to the Engineer   ML 10.3a

Claim No. *
Sub-Clause 10.3 – Interference with Tests on Completion
(Describe which Tests on Completion are under reference)

(Sub-Clause 9.1 describes the Contractor's obligation to programme the execution of the Tests on Completion.)

By our letter (date, reference) we provided you with our proposals and timetable for the execution of the Tests on Completion.

We have been prevented for the last 'x' days (since date …) from carrying out these Tests on Completion due to prevention by the Employer and/or his agents. (Provide a brief description of the cause of prevention.)

Please arrange for the obstruction to be removed without further delay (as we have supervisors/subcontractors/plant now available to carry out these tests).

Yours etc.

Note: If there is no improvement in the situation, the Contractor should consider sending a follow-up letter as indicated below. It is important to note that in some jurisdictions the taking over procedures may differ from and take precedence over the FIDIC standard procedures.

Letter to the Engineer   ML 10.3b

Claim No. *
Sub-Clause 10.3 – Interference with Tests on Completion
(Describe which Tests on Completion are under reference)

(This model letter only has value provided that there are no delays of longer duration caused by the Contractor.)

By our letter (reference, date) we reported interferences by the Employer and/or his agents preventing us from completing the Tests on Completion. (Specify which Tests under reference as appropriate.)

The Tests on Completion have been delayed beyond the programmed dates and have delayed the completion of the Works. In accordance with the provisions of Sub-Clause 10.3, we request you to issue the corresponding Taking Over Certificate with an effective date of … (14 days past programme date). Please advise us when the Tests on Completion can be carried out.

In accordance with the provisions of Sub-Clause 10.3, we consider ourselves entitled to an extension of time, together with reimbursement of our costs plus reasonable profit.

Yours etc.

Note: In these latter stages of the Contract, the extension of time may be particularly significant.

Letter to the Engineer   ML 12.1

Claim No. *
Sub-Clause 12.1 – Works to be Measured

(Final measurements are conventionally signed-off by the Engineer and the Contractor. Should there remain disputes that cannot be readily resolved, the Engineer has the right to issue his measurement unilaterally. The Contractor should forthwith record his disagreement with the Engineer's measurement.)

We have received your measurement sheet (number and description) with which we are in disagreement. Our own measurement sheet is attached for review and is a matter of record. (Give reasoning if not clear from the measurement sheet).

The difference between the measurements are considered by us to be an unpaid item subject to further review and adjustment.

Yours etc.

Letter to the Engineer   ML 12.4

Claim No. *
Sub-Clause 12.4 – Omissions
(Describe the title of omission under reference)

By your letter/instruction/drawing ... (reference, date) we have been instructed to omit (describe work to be omitted), which formed part of the original scope of Works and is not the subject of any replacement work.

We advise you that we have already incurred the following costs (provide detailed listing).

In accordance with the provisions of Sub-Clause 12.4, we hereby request reimbursement of these costs.

Yours etc.

Letter to the Engineer   ML 13.2

<u>Sub-Clause 13.2 – Value Engineering</u>
<u>(Provide title of the proposal)</u>

(Invariably any submission under this heading will follow discussions between the Employer, Engineer and the Contractor.)

We refer to the various discussions between the Parties under the above heading (if it is appropriate, provide a detailed listing of correspondence).

We now enclose our detailed proposal (provide detail) for your consideration. This proposal consists of the following documents (a detailed costing is mandatory).

1.
2.
3.

Please may we have your written agreement to this proposal.

Yours etc.

Letter to the Engineer   ML 13.3

Sub-Clause 13.3 – Variation Procedure
(Request for a Proposal)
(Title of Proposed Variation)

By your letter (date, reference) you have requested a detailed proposal for (title of proposed Variation).

Our detailed proposal is attached and covers the following topics:

- technical proposal including specifications
- effect of the proposed Variation on the Programme
- evaluation of the proposed Variation

We await your further instructions.

Yours etc.

Letter to the Engineer   ML 13.5

Sub-Clause 13.5 – Provisional Sums
(Describe the Title of the Provisional Sum)

(The Engineer is required to specify any works to be carried out by the Contractor (valued as a Variation) and which Plant/Materials/Services are to be provided by a Nominated Subcontractor.)

We refer to your letter (reference, date) instructing us to arrange for the execution of the above works. Our detailed proposal is attached.

(a) For works to be executed by the Contractor, our payment proposals are attached to this letter. (Reference is to be made to Sub-Clause 13.3, particularly if the programme requires modification.)

(b) For works to be executed by the Nominated Subcontractor, we enclose his quotation for your consideration, to which is added a sum of 'x'% for our overhead charges and profit.

Yours etc.

Notes: 1. The overhead percentage should be stated in the Appendix to Tender or otherwise agreed with the Engineer.

2. Care should be taken to include for any direct costs incurred by the Contractor on behalf of the Subcontractor (telephone, accommodation, transport etc.).

Letter to the Engineer   ML 13.6

Sub-Clause 13.6 – Dayworks

(Note: Most dayworks will use the existing resources available to the Contractor on site and the Engineer will not call for quotations. There will be other occasions when the Engineer will require to pre-approve the cost of an expensive item of material such as a valve or similar.)

With reference to your letter of request (reference, date), we enclose herewith a quotation(s) for the supply (and fitting) of (describe material).

Please let us have your further instructions.

Yours etc.

Letter to the Engineer   ML 13.7

Claim No. *
Sub-Clause 13.7 – Adjustments for Changes in Legislation
(Describe briefly the event/occurrence)

In accordance with the provisions of Sub-Clause 13.7, we advise you of the following event/occurrence that represents a change in legislation and entitles us to an adjustment of the Contract Price (provide detail of the event/occurrence under reference with supporting documentation).

We propose to include the value of the adjustment in the next Application for Interim Payment Certificate.

Yours etc.

Letter to the Engineer   ML 14.1d

<u>Sub-Clause 14.1(d) – Breakdown of Lump sums</u>

We enclose herewith our proposed breakdown of the contract lump sum (or parts – describe parts).

Yours etc.

Note: 1. The Engineer does not have to 'approve' this breakdown, but clearly it is preferable if there is an agreement.
       2. The sub-clause does not require a breakdown of unit rates.

Letter to the Engineer   ML 14.2

Sub-Clause 14.2 – Advance Payment Guarantee

We herewith enclose an Advance Payment Guarantee in the sum of (amount) representing 'x'% of the amount to be advanced.

Yours etc.

Letter to the Engineer   ML 14.3a

Sub-Clause 14.3 – Application for Payment of the Advance

We herewith attach our application for the payment of the Advance in accordance with Sub-Clause 14.3.

The Advance Payment Guarantee (Sub-Clause 14.2) and the Performance Security (Sub-Clause 4.2) have been separately provided to the Employer with copy to yourselves, under cover of our letters (reference, date) and (reference, date) respectively.

Yours etc.

Letter to the Engineer   ML 14.3b

Sub-Clause 14.3 – Application for Interim Payment Certificates
Application No.* for the Period Ended (date)

We enclose for your further action six copies of Application No. * for the period ended (date).

This application is accompanied by the following documentation:

1. Progress Report for the month of (date) (Sub-Clause 4.21)
2.
3.

Yours etc.

Letter to the Engineer (optional)   **ML 14.5**

<u>Sub-Clause 14.5 – Plant and Materials Intended for the Works</u>

(It is more appropriate if this topic is dealt with in the preparation of the Application for Interim Payment Certificates and the details included in the documentation provided with the Application.)

We enclose details, calculations and supporting documents relating to Plant and Materials intended for incorporation in the permanent Works as at (date).

These quantities and amounts due will be included in the Application for Interim Payment Certificate No. * for the period ended (date).

Yours etc.

Letter to the Employer   c.c. Engineer   ML 14.8

Sub-Clause 14.8 – Delayed Payment
(Provide reference of Payment Certificate in Delay)

We wish to draw to your attention that payment of Interim Payment No. * for (date) is now in delay. (Clarify if the delay is restricted to one of the contract currencies.)

Application No. * was submitted to the Engineer for his certification on (date). The Engineer has provided his certificate with a date of (date1). Payment was due no later than 56 days after (date1).

Payment was received on (date) 'x' days late (or)

Payment has not yet been received as of the date of this letter.

In accordance with the provisions of Sub-Clause 14.8, we are entitled to receive financing charges compounded monthly at a rate of 3% above the discount rate, both for the local central bank for local currency, and for the foreign central bank for the foreign currency specified in the Contract.

The amounts due at (date) will be calculated and submitted to you for reimbursement. The same will be recorded as an outstanding amount in the next Progress Report.

Yours etc.

Letter to the Engineer   ML 14.10

Sub-Clause 14.10 – Statement at Completion

(To be submitted within 84 days of receipt of the Taking Over Certificate or the last Taking Over if the Works are taken over in sections. The Statement should as far as possible conform to the style of a normal Application for Interim Payment Certificate.)

Please find attached our Statement at Completion in accordance with the requirements of Sub-Clause 14.10.

This statement shows:

(a)   the value of the work done
(b)   details of all further sums due (Claims and other unresolved items)
(c)   an estimate of the value of work yet to be performed

Yours etc.

Letter to the Engineer   ML 14.11

<u>Sub-Clause 14.11 – Application for Final Payment Certificate</u>

(To be submitted within 56 days of receipt of the Performance Certificate.)

Please find attached our Application for Final Payment Certificate showing:

(a) the value of all work done (which will include the value of any claim set-tlements. It will also include the value of work not completed at the date of taking over. The value of outstanding work is now nil since by definition there can be no outstanding works)

(b) details of all further sums due (corresponds to the value of claims yet unresolved)

Yours etc.

Letter to the Engineer   c.c. Employer   ML 14.12

Sub-Clause 14.12 – Discharge

(The form of discharge should be discussed with the Contractor's legal advisor. The following is the recommended form of discharge as given in the FIDIC Contracts Guide.)

We, (name of Contractor), hereby confirm, in the terms of Sub-Clause 14.12 of the Conditions of Contract, that the total of the attached Final Statement, namely (the total value of the Final Statement), represents the full and final settlement of all moneys due to us under or in connection with the Contract. This discharge shall only become effective when we have received the Performance Security and the outstanding balance of this total of the attached Final Statement.

Signed: ……………………..

Letter to the Engineer   c.c. Employer   ML 16.1a

<u>Claim No. *</u>
<u>Sub-Clause 16.1 a – Contractor's Entitlement to Suspend Works</u>
<u>Advance Notice of (Partial) Suspension/Slow-Down of the Works</u>

Payment of the certified amount for interim Certificate(s) No. * was due to be made by no later than (date), being 56 days after our presentation of the corresponding Application to the Engineer. At this date no payment/part payment only has been received. The additional financial costs are the subject of a claim notified by our earlier letter (reference, date).

We now give notice of our intention to suspend the Works in whole or in part or to slow down the progress of the Works within 21 days of your date of receipt of this letter unless the payment is made in the interim.

Yours etc.

Letter to the Engineer   c.c. Employer   ML 16.1b

Claim No. *
Sub-Clause 16.1 a – Contractor's Entitlement to Suspend Works
Notice of (Partial) Suspension/Slow-Down of the Works

Further to our letter (reference, date), we advise you that we have not received payments properly due to us as detailed in that letter.

We now advise you of our intention to suspend partially/slow down the Works (give detail).

In accordance with the provisions of Sub-Clause 16.1, we hereby give notice of our entitlement to an extension of time in respect of any delays incurred, together with payment of our costs plus reasonable profit.

Yours etc.

Appendix J

Letter to the Employer   c.c. Engineer   ML 16.2

Sub-Clause 16.2 – Termination by Contractor

(The following assumes that the most likely cause of termination by the Contractor will be the failure of the Employer to pay the amounts due. Other causes entitling the Contractor to terminate are listed and can be referred to as necessary. Termination will require the advice and direction of an experienced lawyer.)

We refer to our letter (date, reference) addressed to the Engineer and copied to yourselves, on the matter on non-payment to us of the amounts certified by the Engineer.

In accordance with Sub-Clause 16.2(c), we hereby give 14 days' notice of Termination of the Contract. By copy of this letter, we request the Engineer to provide any instructions necessary for the protection of life or property or safety of the Works as stated in Sub-Clause 16.3(a).

Yours etc.

Letter to the Employer   c.c. Engineer   ML 16.3

Sub-Clause 16.3 – Cessation of Work and Removal of Contractor's Equipment

Notice of Termination as given in our letter (reference, date) has now expired.

We have now ceased all work and will now remove from site all our property leaving only those items which have been paid for by you. Thereafter we shall vacate the site.

We take this opportunity to request you to return the Performance Security without delay.

Yours etc.

Letter to the Engineer   c.c. Employer   ML 16.4

<u>Claim No.</u> *
<u>Sub-Clause 16.4 – Payment on Termination</u>

(On termination, the Contractor is entitled to payment in accordance with Sub-Clause 19.6. Once termination is inevitable, the Contractor should commence calculating the amounts due to him using Sub-Clause 19.6 as a guide.)

We attach hereto our valuation of the amounts due to us as a consequence of termination. The valuation has been made in accordance with the principles given in Sub-Clause 19.6.

We request you to issue a Payment Certificate as soon as possible.

Yours etc.

Letter to the Engineer   c.c. Employer   ML 17.3

Claim No. *
Sub-Clause 17.3 – Employer's Risks

(Eight categories of Employer's Risks are identified. Those most likely to be encountered are:

(a)   war and hostilities
(b)   rebellion, revolution
(c)   riot commotion
(h)   unforeseeable forces of nature

If loss or damage occurs to the Works, Goods and the Contractor's Documents, the Contractor shall promptly give notice to the Engineer.)

We wish to inform you that on (date/dates) (describe the event or occurrence referenced to this sub-clause) occurred.

(If there is loss or damage anticipated, add the following sentence:)

We are proceeding to rectify the loss or damage.

We shall keep records of our activities and request you to agree these records with us.

Yours etc.

Letter to the Engineer　　　　　　c.c. Employer　　　　　　ML 17.4

<u>Claim No.</u> *
<u>Sub-Clause 17.4 – Consequences of Employer's Risk</u>
<u>(Give title to event under reference)</u>

Further to our letter (reference, date) informing you of an event or occurrence categorised by Sub-Clause 17.3 – (give Paragraph reference) as an Employer's Risk, it is now clear that it will take time to rectify the loss or damage and we shall incur additional costs.

In accordance with the provisions of Sub-Clause 17.4, we confirm our entitlement to an extension of time, together with reimbursement of our costs (plus reasonable profit in certain cases).

We shall keep records of our activities as a basis for evaluating costs and request you to agree the same with us.

Yours etc.

Letter to the Employer   c.c. Engineer   ML 18.0

<u>Clause 18 – Insurances</u>

We enclose herewith copies of insurances conforming to the requirements of the above clause of the Contract, together with a copy of the premium receipt from the insurer.

Yours etc.

Letter to the Employer   c.c. Engineer   ML 20.2a

<u>Sub-Clause 20.2 – Appointment of the Dispute Adjudication Board</u>
<u>Contractor's Nomination</u>

In accordance with the procedures given in Sub-Clause 20.2, we nominate (name) as a member of the Dispute Adjudication Board.

We enclose the curriculum vitae of (name) for your review, together with a letter from (name), confirming his willingness and availability to take up the appointment.

Yours etc.

Letter to the Employer   c.c. Engineer   ML 20.2b

Sub-Clause 20.2 – Appointment of the Dispute Adjudication Board
Employer's Nomination

With reference to the proposal made in your letter (reference, date), we confirm our acceptance of your proposed candidate, (name), as a member of the Dispute Adjudication Board.

(or)

With reference to the proposal made in your letter (reference, date), we regret to inform you that we are not in agreement with your proposal to appoint (name) as a member of the Dispute Adjudication Board.

Our reasons for rejecting your proposal are (detail to be supplied).

Yours etc.

Letter to the Employer   c.c. Engineer   ML 20.2c

Sub-Clause 20.2 – Appointment of the Dispute Adjudication Board
Nomination of Single Board Member

(Conventionally, the Employer nominates a candidate. The Contractor may either accept or reject the Employer's nomination giving his reasons. The Contractor may propose his own candidate.)

With reference to the proposal made in your letter (reference, date) to appoint (name) as the sole member of the Dispute Adjudication Board, we confirm our acceptance of (name).

(or)

With reference to the proposal made in your letter (reference, date) to appoint (name) as the sole member of the Dispute Adjudication Board, we regret to advise you that we are not in agreement with your proposal (give reasons – lack of qualifications, unsatisfactory performance elsewhere etc.).

We enclose the curriculum vitae of an alternative candidate, (name), for your review, together with a letter from (name), confirming his willingness and availability to take up the appointment.

Yours etc.

Letter to the DAB   c.c. Employer   ML 20.4a

Sub-Clause 20.4 – Obtaining Dispute Adjudication Board's Decision
(Give reference number and title of dispute)

(No matter can be referred to the DAB unless it is a dispute. A dispute will arise if either Party rejects a determination made by the Engineer under Sub-Clause 3.5 or when consultative discussions are clearly not achieving their intended purpose, possibly due to non-cooperation by one of the Parties.)

A dispute has arisen between the Parties in respect of (title and brief description). Following consultative discussions held with the Engineer in accordance with the procedures given in Sub-Clause 3.5, the Engineer issued a determination (reference) on (date).

By letter (reference, date) we registered our rejection of the Engineer's determination, a copy of which is attached, together with a copy of the Engineer's determination. (Provide brief statement of what is in dispute.)

In accordance with the provisions of Sub-Clause 20.4 of the General Conditions of Contract, we hereby refer the dispute to the DAB for the purpose of their making a decision on the dispute.

'X' copies of our detailed request are attached (or) will be submitted under separate cover.

Yours etc.

Letter to the Employer   c.c. Engineer   ML 20.4b

Sub-Clause 20.4 – Obtaining Dispute Adjudication Board's Decision
(Give reference number and title of dispute)
DAB Decision Dated (….)

We received the decision of the DAB in respect of the above dispute on (date).

We are dissatisfied with the decision of the DAB and give notice that we intend to refer the dispute to arbitration in accordance with the provisions of Sub-Clause 20.6 of the General Conditions of Contract.

Yours etc.

Letter to the Employer   c.c. Engineer   ML 20.5

Sub-Clause 20.5 – Amicable Settlement
(Give reference number and title of dispute)
Amicable Settlement

By letter (reference, date) we gave notice of dissatisfaction with the decision of the DAB and informed you of our intention to refer the dispute to arbitration.

In accordance with the procedures described in Sub-Clause 20.5 'Amicable Settlement' of the General Conditions of Contract, it is required that the Parties attempt to resolve the dispute amicably.

Please inform us when we can meet with you in an attempt to achieve an amicable settlement.

Yours etc.

Note: 1. The Contract allows a period of 56 days to achieve amicable settlement, otherwise the dispute can be referred directly to arbitration.
2. Ensure that any relevant discussions between the Parties are clearly referenced to Sub-Clause 20.5 and that detailed records are maintained of any discussions and decisions reached – all to be agreed in writing.

Introduction to indexes

In the preparation of the 'Rainbow' series of Conditions of Contract and the FIDIC Contracts Guide, FIDIC provides an Index which sorts the contents of the various Clauses and Sub-Clauses according to topics and not necessarily in conformity with the printed formal titles of the Clauses and Sub-Clauses.

For example, Sub-Clause 1.3 is titled 'Communications' and yet in the Index the following references can be located (each with a reference to this Sub-Clause):

Addresses for Communications
Certificates, copies to be sent
Communications
Electronic Transmission of Communications
Notices, Addresses for Communications

There is a significant number of similar multiple references for other Clauses and Sub-Clauses.

The FIDIC Index system is undoubtedly very comprehensive and of considerable benefit to those who are not familiar with the contents of the FIDIC Conditions of Contract and have only key topic references with which to work.

In this book the original FIDIC index system has been expanded to provide appropriate reference to the full text of this book and yet retains the possibility of referencing the text of other related FIDIC documents, notably the FIDIC Contracts Guide, which use the same index system.

However, there are occasions when it would be convenient to have available an alternative index that would sort topics according to the clause numbering and descriptions used by FIDIC. An alternative form of index is provided for this purpose.

A Contractor's Guide to the FIDIC Conditions of Contract, First Edition. Michael D. Robinson.
© 2011 John Wiley & Sons, Ltd. Published 2011 by John Wiley & Sons, Ltd.

Index of sub-clauses (FIDIC system)

A Contractor's Guide to the FIDIC Conditions of Contract, First Edition. Michael D. Robinson.
© 2011 John Wiley & Sons, Ltd. Published 2011 by John Wiley & Sons, Ltd.

Index of sub-clauses (sorted according to FIDIC clause numbering system)

A Contractor's Guide to the FIDIC Conditions of Contract, First Edition. Michael D. Robinson.
© 2011 John Wiley & Sons, Ltd. Published 2011 by John Wiley & Sons, Ltd.